The Country Commonplace Book

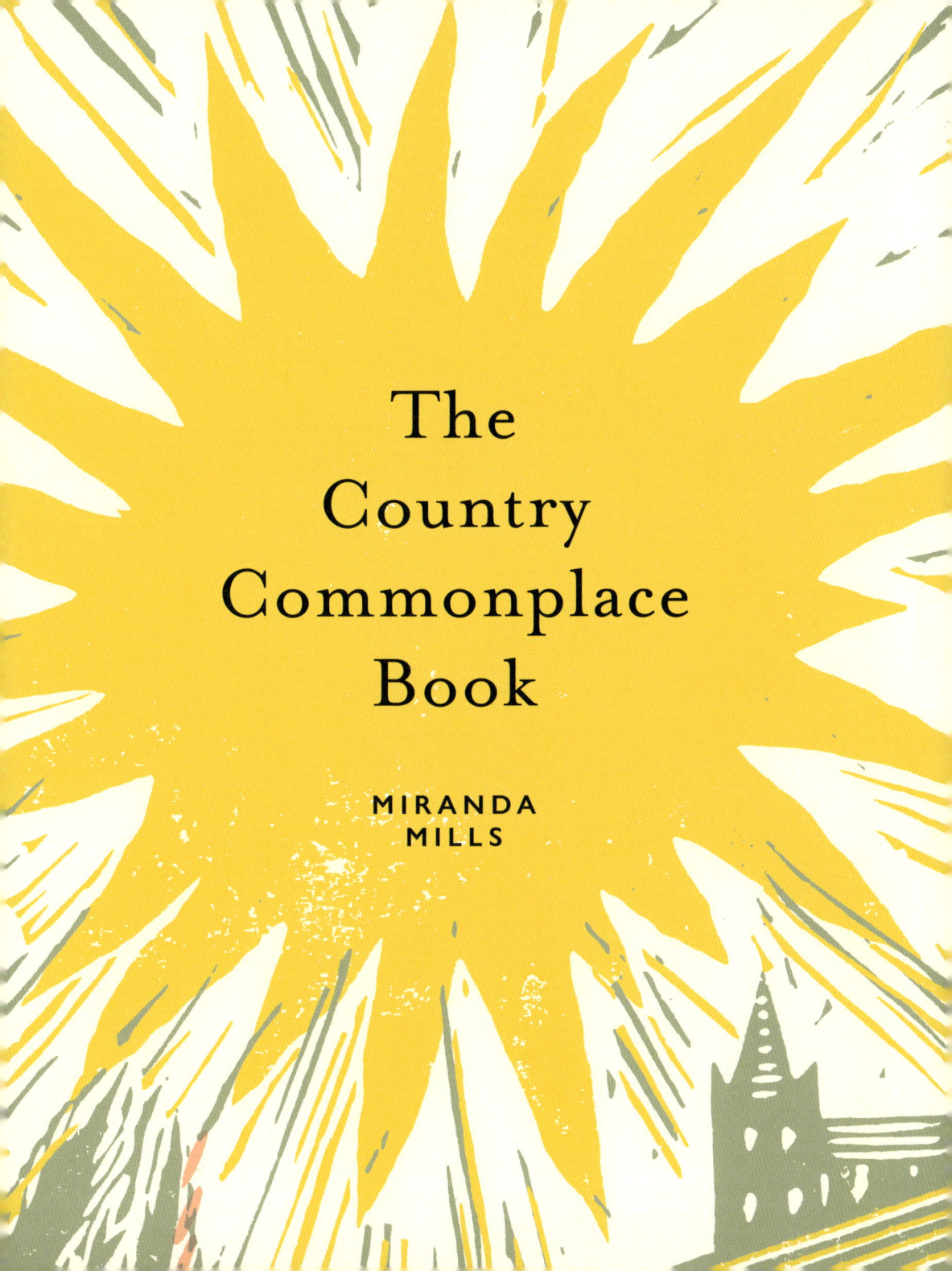

For my Mum, with all my love.

First published in the United Kingdom in 2025 by
Batsford
43 Great Ormond Street
London
WC1N 3HZ

An imprint of B. T. Batsford Holdings Limited

Copyright © B. T. Batsford Ltd 2025
Text copyright © Miranda Mills 2025

Illustrations reproduced from linocuts by Debbie Powell

All rights reserved. No part of this publication may be copied, displayed, extracted, reproduced, utilized, stored in a retrieval system or transmitted in any form or by any means, electronic, mechanical or otherwise including but not limited to photocopying, recording, or scanning without the prior written permission of the publishers.

ISBN 978 1 84994 999 6

A CIP catalogue record for this book is available from the British Library.

10 9 8 7 6 5 4 3 2

Reproduction by Mission Productions, Hong Kong
Printed by IMAK Ofset, Turkey

This book can be ordered direct from the publisher at www.batsfordbooks.com, or try your local bookshop

Distributed throughout the UK and Europe by Abrams & Chronicle Books, 1 West Smithfield, London EC1A 9JU and 57 rue Gaston Tessier, 75166 Paris, France

www.abramsandchronicle.co.uk
info@abramsandchronicle.co.uk

CONTENTS

INTRODUCTION	6
SPRING	**12**
SUMMER	**70**
AUTUMN	**128**
WINTER	**186**
INDEX	244
SOURCES	251
ACKNOWLEDGEMENTS	256
ABOUT THE AUTHOR	256

WHAT IS A COMMONPLACE BOOK?

Commonplace books are a type of journal used to record favourite quotes, excerpts from books, poems, anecdotes, proverbs, wise sayings, lists, recipes, prayers and song lyrics.

For anyone who loves language and literature, a commonplace book is an invaluable resource. Unlike diaries or other forms of journaling, commonplace books are not generally used to capture your original thoughts or details of day-to-day life. Instead, a commonplace book is a place to record any writing that you particularly want to remember: a poem that made your heart soar, a clever turn of phrase or an evocative piece of prose.

If the idea of journaling appeals to you, but you're someone who has struggled to write consistently in a diary, then a commonplace book may be a great option. Often, a commonplace book is kept over many years, only added to when a new nugget of literary gold is found.

For years, I kept a commonplace book without realizing it, and I suspect that's true of many people. If you have a notebook in which you collect favourite quotes, then you already have a commonplace book. You're in good company! Commonplacing has been popular for centuries, and many great writers and thinkers have kept a commonplace book, including John Milton, George Eliot, Charles Dodgson (better known as Lewis Carroll), Virginia Woolf, E. M. Forster, W. H. Auden, Oscar Wilde and Octavia Butler.

THE HISTORY OF THE COMMONPLACE BOOK

In the early 16th century, the Dutch priest, writer and educationalist, Erasmus (c. 1466–1536), popularized the practice of note-taking in Europe. He encouraged his students to read from a range of authors to broaden their knowledge and to select, organize and write down quotations, opinions, proverbs and excerpts in an effort to aid their own reasoning powers and debating skills.

Throughout early modern times, the habit of keeping a commonplace book became more widespread, especially as paper became cheaper and easier to obtain. The English philosopher John Locke (1632–1704) published a book that explained his system for organizing and categorizing a commonplace book. By this time, the habit of commonplacing had moved beyond scholars and students, who initially used commonplace books to aid their studies. People, for example, might use their commonplace books in church to write down memorable lines from sermons.

In the late 18th century, commercial commonplace books were published in response to their popularity. The bookseller and publisher John Bell (1745–1831) issued a printed commonplace book, 'form'd generally upon the principles recommended and practised by Mr. Locke', which left plenty of blank pages for people to fill in themselves. A few of these commonplace books, written in by their owners, are held at the British Library and offer a fascinating insight into the history of commonplacing. Although the popularity of commonplace books began to dwindle in the 19th and 20th centuries, they were still used as a means to store information and inspiration.

In recent years, there's been a rekindling of interest in commonplacing, perhaps in response to our highly digitized world, and I hope this interest continues to grow as more people discover the joy of commonplacing.

HOW TO KEEP A COMMONPLACE BOOK

There is no wrong way to keep a commonplace book, which is a large part of the fun. Commonplacing is an individual practice, and I encourage you to keep a commonplace book in whatever form most appeals to you.

Some people choose to use a digital note-taking or journaling app, but I must admit that I love the sensory delights that a physical notebook and fountain pen offer. Choosing to handwrite rather than type means I'm forced to slow down and pay attention to each word I'm writing. This slow practice helps me to internalize the beautiful lines I'm copying out.

However, in order to capture quotes quickly, modern technology has many advantages. I often use my phone to take a photo of a page from a book I'm reading, or I screenshot a terrific quote shared on social media. Then, at some point in the week, I'll take the time to transfer these quotes into my physical commonplace book.

In general, I like to order commonplace books chronologically, so my entries directly reflect my interests and my reading through each month and year. In this way, my commonplace book is a type

of diary, and I enjoy looking back on entries and remembering the books and poems I discovered at certain points in my life.

Many people choose to categorize their commonplace entries under certain headings or themes. You may even decide to devote an entire commonplace book to a single subject, just as *The Country Commonplace Book* is devoted to country life and country pleasures throughout the seasons. A commonplace book can help you to organize notes, inspiration and ideas around a particular project. George Eliot, for example, kept commonplace books for novels that she wrote. Eliot sketched examples of country hats and bonnets that were popular at the time in which her novel, *Adam Bede*, was set, to assist her descriptions of her characters' clothing. She also copied out quotations that inspired her when formulating her ideas for *Middlemarch*.

It's unnecessary to confine yourself to words in your commonplace book; like George Eliot, you may want to include some sketches, or perhaps interesting cuttings from magazines and newspapers. I'm not an artist, but I like to include postcards of artworks I admire within the pages of my commonplace book.

If you decide to keep a commonplace book, I hope it becomes a treasured source of inspiration and wisdom for you.

THE COUNTRY COMMONPLACE BOOK

The Country Commonplace Book is organized by the seasons, with excerpts of country writing, nature poems, seasonal reading lists, recipes from my country kitchen, country lore and word lists divided between the four sections.

When I moved to the Yorkshire countryside after living in London for over a decade, I was surprised to realize I was a true country girl at heart. As I discovered the beautiful landscape and garden around my home, I witnessed the changes that each season brought, from snowdrops in winter to ripe raspberries in summer. Always a bibliophile, I started to fill my bookshelves with more nature writing and poetry anthologies, relishing the exquisite language of great writers that expressed the joy and beauty (as well as the hardships) of country life. In general, I paid more attention to descriptions of the countryside in novels I read, and noted down my favourite passages, many of which are included here.

The Country Commonplace Book brings together poems and excerpts I have read and loved, and I hope you will find this book a welcome companion to each season of the year. Whether living in the city or the country, I believe deepening our connection to nature is vital for our mental, physical and spiritual wellbeing.

Immersing myself in the language and writing of the countryside taught me to slow down so that I could better observe and appreciate the natural landscape surrounding me. In our hectic lives, so often we forget to pay attention to what is happening around us. As Edward Thomas expresses in his poem 'First Known When Lost', how sad it is to awaken to the presence – let alone the importance – of something only by its absence. So much has been lost from the countryside already: the sound of the cuckoo heralding summer I have very rarely heard since moving to

Yorkshire, but – as is clear from the traditional songs and excerpts I've included in this book – this call was once a ubiquitous part of the British country soundscape in spring.

I have designed *The Country Commonplace Book* so that it may be simply read and enjoyed as a type of anthology, but if you're inspired to start a commonplace book, I would be thrilled if one or two quotes from this book find their way into yours and start you off on your own commonplacing journey. More than anything, I hope the words I've selected will encourage you, too, to slow down, pay attention and appreciate the beauty of the world around you.

We are wildflowers
Wild as the wind
Wild as the dawn
Wild within

    Lemn Sissay (1967–)

from THE LAND

The country habit has me by the heart,
For he's bewitched forever who has seen,
Not with his eyes but with his vision, Spring
Flow down the woods and stipple leaves with sun,
As each man knows the life that fits him best,
The shape it makes in his soul, the tune, the tone,
And after ranging on a tentative flight
Stoops like the merlin to the constant lure.
The country habit has me by the heart.

VITA SACKVILLE-WEST (1892–1962)

THE SHEPHERD

How sweet is the shepherd's sweet lot!
From the morn to the evening he strays;
He shall follow his sheep all the day,
And his tongue shall be filled with praise.

For he hears the lambs' innocent call,
And he hears the ewes' tender reply;
He is watchful while they are in peace,
For they know when their shepherd is nigh.

                    WILLIAM BLAKE (1757—1827)

On a mild sunny morning—rather soft under foot; for the last fall of snow was only just wasted away, leaving yet a thin ridge, here and there, lingering on the fresh green grass beneath the hedges; but beside them already, the young primroses were peeping from among their moist, dark foliage, and the lark above was singing of summer, and hope, and love, and every heavenly thing—I was out on the hill-side, enjoying these delights, and looking after the well-being of my young lambs and their mothers…

Anne Brontë (1820–1849), from
The Tenant of Wildfell Hall, 1848

It was now early spring—the time of going to grass with the sheep, when they have the first feed of the meadows, before these are laid up for mowing. The wind, which had been blowing east for several weeks, had veered to the southward, and the middle of spring had come abruptly—almost without a beginning. It was that period in the vernal quarter when we may suppose the Dryads to be waking for the season. The vegetable world begins to move and swell and the saps to rise…

Thomas Hardy (1840–1928), from
Far from the Madding Crowd, 1874

Spring was moving in the air above and in the earth below and around him, penetrating even his dark and lowly little house with its spirit of divine discontent and longing.

Kenneth Grahame (1859–1932), from
The Wind in the Willows, 1908

LINES WRITTEN IN EARLY SPRING

I heard a thousand blended notes,
While in a grove I sate reclined,
In that sweet mood when pleasant thoughts
Bring sad thoughts to the mind.

To her fair works did Nature link
The human soul that through me ran;
And much it grieved my heart to think
What man has made of man.

Through primrose tufts, in that green bower,
The periwinkle trailed its wreaths;
And 'tis my faith that every flower
Enjoys the air it breathes.

The birds around me hopped and played,
Their thoughts I cannot measure:—
But the least motion which they made
It seemed a thrill of pleasure.

The budding twigs spread out their fan,
To catch the breezy air;
And I must think, do all I can,
That there was pleasure there.

If this belief from heaven be sent,
If such be Nature's holy plan,
Have I not reason to lament
What man has made of man?

                William Wordsworth (1770–1850)

Wednesday, 8th March.–Very pleasant day; quite spring-like. The snow is melting fast. Spring in the *air*, in the *light*, and in the *sky*, although the earth is yet unconscious of its approach. We have weather as mild as this in December, but there is something in the fulness and softness of the light beaming in the sky this morning which tells of spring,—the early dawn before the summer day. A little downy woodpecker and a bluejay were running about the apple-trees hunting for insects; we watched them awhile with interest, for few birds are seen here during the winter.

Susan Fenimore Cooper (1813–1894), from *Rural Hours*, 1850

The first sparrow of spring! The year beginning with younger hope than ever! The faint silvery warblings heard over the partially bare and moist fields from the blue-bird, the song-sparrow, and the red-wing, as if the last flakes of winter tinkled as they fell! What at such a time are histories, chronologies, traditions, and all written revelations? The brooks sing carols and glees to the spring. The marsh-hawk sailing low over the meadow is already seeking the first slimy life that awakes. The sinking sound of melting snow is heard in all dells, and the ice dissolves apace in the ponds. The grass flames up on the hillsides like a spring fire,—'et primitus oritur herba imbribus primoribus evocata,'—as if the earth sent forth an inward heat to greet the returning sun; not yellow but green is the color of its flame;—the symbol of perpetual youth, the grass-blade, like a long green ribbon, streams from the sod into the summer, checked indeed by the frost, but anon pushing on again, lifting its spear of last year's hay with the fresh life below.

Henry David Thoreau (1817–1862), from *Walden*, 1854

They bought a gardening book—and spent the evening over it. In the kitchen. You tend to sit in the kitchen when it is very light and clean, bright with gay-coloured crockery and sparkling with silvery tinsmith's work… Especially when the kitchen window looks out on the back garden, where the fruit trees are near blossom…. A very happy evening they spent over the gardening book. Lucilla made a list of the seeds that would be wanted to carry out what was really a quite brilliant scheme for a year's flower-growing.

                Edith Nesbit (1858–1924), from *The Lark*, 1922

Spring, that year, came delicately in among the Galway hills; in primroses, in wild bursts of gorse, and in the later snow of hawthorn, unbeaten by the rain or the wet west wind of rougher seasons. A cuckoo had dropped out of space into the copse at the back of Gurthnamuckla, and kept calling there with a lusty sweetness; a mist of green was breathed upon the trees, and in the meadows by the lake a corncrake was adding a diffident guttural or two to the chirruping chorus of coots and moorhens.

                Edith Somerville (1858–1949) and Violet Florence Martin
                (1862–1915), writing as 'Somerville & Ross', from
                The Real Charlotte, 1894

Daffodils,
    That come before the swallow dares, and take
    The winds of March with beauty…

                William Shakespeare (1564–1616), from *The Winter's Tale*, 1623

LIFE MASK

When the senses come back in the morning,
the nose is a mouth full of spring:
the mouth is an earful of birdsong;
the eyes are lips on the camomile lawn;
the ear is an eye of calm blue sky.

When the broken heart begins to mind,
the heart is a bird with a tender wing,
the tears are pear blossom blossoming,
the shaken love grows green shining leaves,
the throat doesn't close, it is opening

like a long necked swan in the morning,
like the sea and the river meeting,
like the huge heron's soaring wings:
I sat up with my pale face in my hands
And all of a sudden it was spring.

                    Jackie Kay (1961–)

RHUBARB GIN

A delicious, simple recipe for the pink forced rhubarb that appears early in spring.

Makes about 750ml

INGREDIENTS

350g (12oz) rhubarb stalks

180g (6¼oz) caster sugar

750ml (25⅓fl oz) gin (use a good quality, but not overly expensive or highly flavoured London Dry style gin)

2 lemon peels

YOU WILL NEED

1 x 1 litre (35fl oz) lidded, sterilized glass jar with a seal

1 x fine mesh sieve

1 x small funnel

3 x 250ml (9fl oz) sealable glass bottles

METHOD

1. Cut the prepared rhubarb stalks into approximately 2.5cm (1 inch) chunks and layer in the sterilized glass jar with the caster sugar.

2. Add the gin and lemon peels and seal the jar.

3. Shake the jar to mix the ingredients together.

4. Place in a dark larder or cupboard and turn the jar every other day until you can see that the sugar has dissolved.

5. Leave the jar alone for 1 month and then strain through a fine mesh sieve into a clean jug.

6. Using a small funnel, pour the gin into the clean glass bottles and seal.

7. The bottles can be stored in a cupboard or drinks cabinet or chilled in the fridge, and the gin can be used immediately in cocktails. A bottle makes a lovely gift for friends and neighbours too!

I might mention all the divine charms of a bright spring day, but if you had never in your life utterly forgotten yourself in straining your eyes after the mounting lark, or in wandering through the still lanes when the fresh-opened blossoms fill them with a sacred silent beauty like that of fretted aisles, where would be the use of my descriptive catalogue? I could never make you know what I meant by a bright spring day.

George Eliot (1819–1880), from *Adam Bede*, 1859

It was sad to Fanny to lose all the pleasures of spring. She had not known before what pleasures she *had* to lose in passing March and April in a town. She had not known before how much the beginnings and progress of vegetation had delighted her. What animation, both of body and mind, she had derived from watching the advance of that season which cannot, in spite of its capriciousness, be unlovely, and seeing its increasing beauties from the earliest flowers in the warmest divisions of her aunt's garden, to the opening of leaves of her uncle's plantations, and the glory of his woods. To be losing such pleasures was no trifle…

Jane Austen (1775–1817), from *Mansfield Park*, 1814

Spring weather came on rather suddenly, the unsealing of buds that had long been swollen accomplishing itself in the space of one warm night. The rush of sap in the veins of the trees could almost be heard… In-door people said they had heard the nightingale, to which out-door people replied contemptuously that they had heard him a fortnight before.

Thomas Hardy (1840–1928), from *The Woodlanders*, 1887

ON THE FIRST FLOWERS OF SPRING

The thrush is building a nest
right outside your bedroom window,

and the freshly thawed breeze
brings hope into your now green garden.

The flowers you planted last year
sing in yellow and pink blooms.

Spring and you are soulmates,
life blossoming everywhere for you,

filled with healing and promise.

    Nikita Gill (1987–)

from INVITATION TO THE COUNTRY

Now 'tis Spring on wood and wold,
Early Spring that shivers with cold,
But gladdens, and gathers, day by day,
A lovelier hue, a warmer ray,
A sweeter song, a dearer ditty;
Ouzel and throstle, new-mated and gay,
Singing their bridals on every spray—
Oh, hear them, deep in the songless City!
Cast off the yoke of toil and smoke,
As Spring is casting winter's grey,
As serpents cast their skins away:
And come, for the Country awaits thee with pity
And longs to bathe thee in her delight,
And take a new joy in thy kindling sight;
And I no less, by day and night,
Long for thy coming, and watch for, and wait thee,
And wonder what duties can thus berate thee...

Primrose tufts peep over the brooks,
Fair faces amid moist decay!
The rivulets run with the dead leaves at play,
The leafless elms are alive with the rooks.

Over the meadows the cowslips are springing,
The marshes are thick with king-cup gold,
Clear is the cry of the lambs in the fold,
The skylark is singing, and singing, and singing.

GEORGE MEREDITH (1828—1909)

WHEN GREEN BUDS HANG IN THE ELM LIKE DUST

When green buds hang in the elm like dust
    And sprinkle the lime like rain,
Forth I wander, forth I must,
    And drink of life again.
Forth I must by hedgerow bowers
    To look at the leaves uncurled,
And stand in the fields where cuckoo-flowers
    Are lying about the world.

A. E. Housman (1859–1936)

I WANDERED LONELY AS A CLOUD

I wandered lonely as a cloud
That floats on high o'er vales and hills,
When all at once I saw a crowd,
A host, of golden daffodils;
Beside the lake, beneath the trees,
Fluttering and dancing in the breeze.

Continuous as the stars that shine
And twinkle on the milky way,
They stretched in never-ending line
Along the margin of a bay:
Ten thousand saw I at a glance,
Tossing their heads in sprightly dance.

The waves beside them danced; but they
Out-did the sparkling waves in glee:
A poet could not but be gay,
In such a jocund company:
I gazed—and gazed—but little thought
What wealth the show to me had brought:

For oft, when on my couch I lie
In vacant or in pensive mood,
They flash upon that inward eye
Which is the bliss of solitude;
And then my heart with pleasure fills,
And dances with the daffodils.

William Wordsworth (1770–1850)

But the glory of the copse just now consists in the great stretches of Daffodils. Through the wood run shallow, parallel hollows, the lowest part of each depression some nine paces apart. Local tradition says they are the remains of old pack-horse roads… Where these pass through the birch copse the Daffodils have been planted in the shallow hollows of the old ways, in spaces of some three yards broad by thirty or forty yards long—one kind at a time. Two of such tracks, planted with *Narcissus princeps* and *N. Horsfieldi*, are now waving rivers of bloom, in many lights and accidents of cloud and sunshine full of pictorial effect.

    Gertrude Jekyll (1843–1932), from *Wood and Garden*, 1899

When we were in the woods beyond Gowbarrow park we saw a few daffodils close to the water-side. We fancied that the lake had floated the seeds ashore, and that the little colony had so sprung up. But as we went along there were more and yet more; and at last, under the boughs of the trees, we saw that there was a long belt of them along the shore, about the breadth of a country turnpike road. I never saw daffodils so beautiful. They grew among the mossy stones about and about them; some rested their heads upon these stones as on a pillow for weariness; and the rest tossed and reeled and danced, and seemed as if they verily laughed with the wind, that blew upon them over the lake; they looked so gay, ever glancing, ever changing. This wind blew directly over the lake to them. There was here and there a little knot, and a few stragglers a few yards higher up; but they were so few as not to disturb the simplicity, unity, and life of that one busy highway.

    Dorothy Wordsworth (1771–1855), Thursday 15 April 1802

All along the lane to our house in Wales the banks are still covered in primroses and violets, which have now been joined by the greater stitchwort, ground ivy and cuckoo flower. I know this because we grew ashamed of our ignorance and so spent many hours drifting up and down with a book identifying everything that showed its face. It is exquisitely pleasurable to be able to tell a visitor from the city that that little pink flower is not red campion as he might have supposed but herb-robert because the one has basal stalks and oval leaves and the other has triangular, 1–2 pinnated leaves.

    Alice Thomas Ellis (1932–2005), from *Home Life*, 1986

One warm spring day, Vance Weston strode along between the ruts, past squares of Swedish market-gardening and raw pastures waiting for the boom. These were the days when he liked the expectancy of Crampton better than the completeness of Euphoria — days of the sudden prairie spring, when the lilacs in his grandmother's dooryard were bursting, and the maples by the river fringing themselves with rosy keys, when the earth throbbed with renewal and the heavy white clouds moved across the sky like flocks of teeming ewes. In a clump of trees near the road a bird began over and over its low tentative song, and in the ditches a glossy-leaved weed, nameless to Vance, spangled the mud with golden chalices. He felt a passionate desire to embrace the budding earth and everything that stirred and swelled in it. He was irritated by the fact that he did not know the name of the bird, or of the yellow flowers. 'I should like to give everything its right name, and to know why that name was the right one,' he thought; the names of things had always seemed to him as closely and mysteriously a part of them as his skin or eyelashes of himself.

    Edith Wharton (1862–1937), from *Hudson River Bracketed*, 1929

LETTER FROM TOWN:
THE ALMOND TREE

You promised to send me some violets. Did you forget?
  White ones and blue ones from under the orchard hedge?
  Sweet dark purple, and white ones mixed for a pledge
Of our early love that hardly has opened yet.

Here there's an almond tree—you have never seen
  Such a one in the north—it flowers on the street, and I stand
  Every day by the fence to look up for the flowers that expand
At rest in the blue, and wonder at what they mean.

Under the almond tree, the happy lands
  Provence, Japan, and Italy repose,
  And passing feet are chatter and clapping of those
Who play around us, country girls clapping their hands.

You, my love, the foremost, in a flowered gown,
  All your unbearable tenderness, you with the laughter
  Startled upon your eyes now so wide with hereafter,
You with loose hands of abandonment hanging down.

                        D. H. LAWRENCE (1885—1930)

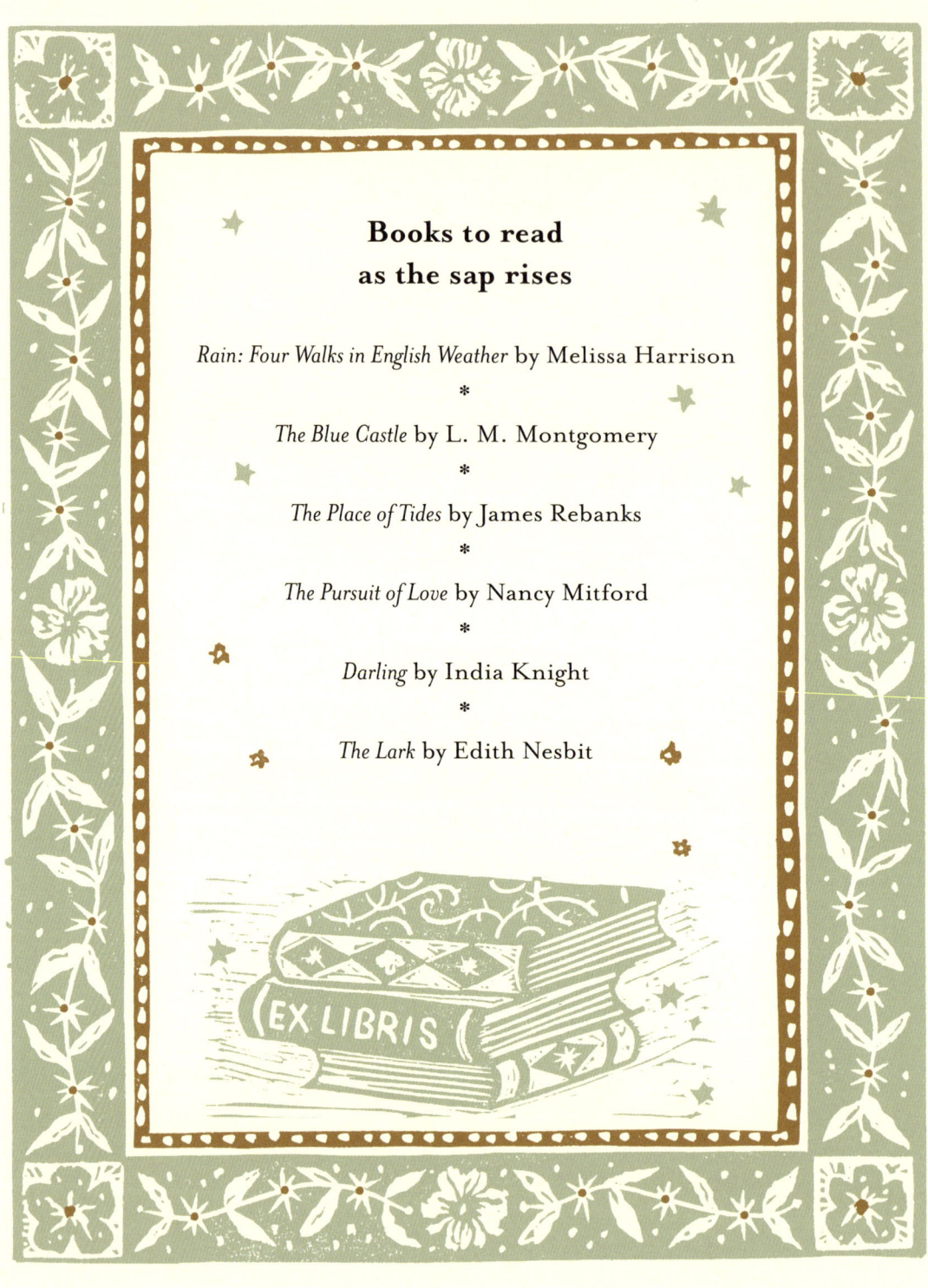

Books to read as the sap rises

Rain: Four Walks in English Weather by Melissa Harrison

*

The Blue Castle by L. M. Montgomery

*

The Place of Tides by James Rebanks

*

The Pursuit of Love by Nancy Mitford

*

Darling by India Knight

*

The Lark by Edith Nesbit

Now a few yards farther, and I reach the bank. Ah! I smell them already—their exquisite perfume steams and lingers in this moist, heavy air. Through this little gate, and along the green south bank of this green wheat-field, and they burst upon me, the lovely violets, in tenfold loveliness. The ground is covered with them, white and purple, enamelling the short dewy grass, looking but the more vividly coloured under the dull, leaden sky. There they lie by hundreds, by thousands… How beautifully they are placed too, on this sloping bank, with the palm branches waving over them, full of early bees, and mixing their honeyed scent with the more delicate violet odour! How transparent and smooth and lusty are the branches, full of sap and life! And there, just by the old mossy root, is a superb tuft of primroses, with a yellow butterfly hovering over them, like a flower floating on the air.

Mary Russell Mitford (1787–1855), from *Our Village*, 1824

Of all the cooing notes of the different species I am acquainted with, that of the stock-dove, a pigeon with no set song, is undoubtedly the most attractive: next in order is that of the wood-pigeon on account of its depth and human-like character. And it is far from monotonous. In this wood in March I have often kept near a pigeon for half an hour at a time hearing it uttering its cooing note, repeated half a dozen or more times, at intervals of three or four minutes; and again and again the note has changed in length and power and modulation. In the profound stillness, on a windless day, of the vast beechen woods, these sonorous notes had a singularly beautiful effect.

W. H. Hudson (1841–1922), from *Birds and Man*, 1920

PLANT A TREE

He who plants a tree
    Plants a hope.
    Rootlets up through fibres blindly grope;
Leaves unfold into horizons free.
    So man's life must climb
    From the clods of time
    Unto heavens sublime.
Canst thou prophesy, thou little tree,
What the glory of thy boughs shall be?

He who plants a tree
    Plants a joy;
    Plants a comfort that will never cloy;
Every day a fresh reality,
    Beautiful and strong,
    To whose shelter throng
    Creatures blithe with song.
If thou couldst but know, thou happy tree,
Of the bliss that shall inhabit thee!

He who plants a tree,—
    He plants peace.
    Under its green curtains jargons cease.
Leaf and zephyr murmur soothingly;
    Shadows soft with sleep

    Down tired eyelids creep,
       Balm of slumber deep.
Never has thou dreamed, thou blessèd tree,
Of the benediction thou shalt be.

He who plants a tree,—
       He plants youth;
       Vigor won for centuries in sooth;
Life of time, that hints eternity!
       Boughs their strength uprear:
       New shoots, every year,
       On old growths appear;
Thou shalt teach the ages, sturdy tree,
Youth of soul is immortality.

He who plants a tree,—
       He plants love,
       Tents of coolness spreading out above
Wayfarers he may not live to see.
       Gifts that grow are best;
       Hands that bless are blest;
       Plant! life does the rest!
Heaven and earth help him who plants a tree,
And his work its own reward shall be.

                        Lucy Larcom (1824–1893)

The hill fills nearly half the sky, and just above it stands the white full moon, as one who looks over his lands. It warms the low, pale, curdled sky, but does not disturb the darkness of the beeches. All its light seems to fall and settle, as if it would dwell there for ever in the cherry trees on either hand. All are blossoming, and in their branches the nightingales sing out of the blossom…

Edward Thomas (1878–1917), from *The Heart of England*, 1906

A huge cherry-tree grew outside, so close that its boughs tapped against the house, and it was so thick-set with blossoms that hardly a leaf was to be seen. On both sides of the house was a big orchard, one of apple-trees and one of cherry-trees, also showered over with blossoms; and their grass was all sprinkled with dandelions. In the garden below were lilac-trees purple with flowers, and their dizzily sweet fragrance drifted up to the window on the morning wind.

Below the garden a green field lush with clover sloped down to the hollow where the brook ran and where scores of white birches grew, upspringing airily out of an undergrowth suggestive of delightful possibilities in ferns and mosses and woodsy things generally. Beyond it was a hill, green and feathery with spruce and fir; there was a gap in it where the gray gable end of the little house she had seen from the other side of the Lake of Shining Waters was visible.

Off to the left were the big barns and beyond them, away down over green, low-sloping fields, was a sparkling blue glimpse of sea.

Anne's beauty-loving eyes lingered on it all, taking everything greedily in. She had looked on so many unlovely places in her life, poor child; but this was as lovely as anything she had ever dreamed.

L. M. Montgomery (1874–1942), from *Anne of Green Gables*, 1908

PREPARATION

The little bird sits in the nest and sings
   A shy, soft song to the morning light;
And it flutters a little and prunes its wings.
     The song is halting and poor and brief,
     And the fluttering wings scarce stir a leaf;
But the note is a prelude to sweeter things,
   And the busy bill and the flutter slight
   Are proving the wings for a bolder flight!

PAUL LAURENCE DUNBAR (1872—1906)

The orchard consisted of about a score of old apple and plum trees on a square of rough grass at the bottom of the garden, beyond which ran the small, sluggish stream, half choked with rushes and bordered with willows. Laura, who had felt so tired before, suddenly felt tired no more, but ran and shouted and played 'tig' with the others around the tree trunks. The apple blossom was nearly over and the petals were falling and they all tried to catch a petal or two because one of the cousins said that for every petal they caught they would have a happy month. Then there were small green gooseberries to crunch and forget-me-nots to pick.

Flora Thompson (1876–1947), from *Over to Candleford*, 1941

An old lady had an Alderney cow, which she looked upon as a daughter. You could not pay the short quarter of an hour call without being told of the wonderful milk or wonderful intelligence of this animal. The whole town knew and kindly regarded Miss Betsy Barker's Alderney; therefore great was the sympathy and regret when, in an unguarded moment, the poor cow tumbled into a lime-pit. She moaned so loudly that she was soon heard and rescued; but meanwhile the poor beast had lost most of her hair, and came out looking naked, cold, and miserable, in a bare skin. Everybody pitied the animal, though a few could not restrain their smiles at her droll appearance. Miss Betsy Barker absolutely cried with sorrow and dismay; and it was said she thought of trying a bath of oil. This remedy, perhaps, was recommended by some one of the number whose advice she asked; but the proposal, if ever it was made, was knocked on the head by Captain Brown's decided 'Get her a flannel waistcoat and flannel drawers, ma'am, if you wish to keep her alive. But my advice is, kill the poor creature at once.'

Miss Betsy Barker dried her eyes, and thanked the Captain heartily; she set to work, and by-and-by all the town turned out to see the Alderney meekly going to her pasture, clad in dark grey flannel. I have watched her myself many a time. Do you ever see cows dressed in grey flannel in London?

Elizabeth Gaskell (1810–1865), from *Cranford*, 1853

My two large Piggs, by drinking some Beer grounds taking out of one of my Barrels today, got so amazingly drunk by it, that they were not able to stand and appeared like dead things almost, and so remained all night from dinner time today. I never saw Piggs so drunk in my life….

James Woodforde (1740–1803), 15 April 1778

We breakfasted, dined and supped and slept again at home. My 2 Piggs are still unable to walk yet, but they are better than they were yesterday. They tumble about the yard and can by no means stand at all steady yet. In the afternoon my 2 Piggs were tolerably sober.

James Woodforde (1740–1803), 16 April 1778

To-day is completely April;— clouds and sunshine, wind and showers; blossoms on the trees, grass in the fields, swallows by the ponds, snakes in the hedgerows, nightingales in the thickets, and cuckoos everywhere.

Mary Russell Mitford (1787–1855), from *Our Village*, 1824

SOWING

It was a perfect day
For sowing; just
As sweet and dry was the ground
As tobacco-dust.

I tasted deep the hour
Between the far
Owl's chuckling first soft cry
And the first star.

A long stretched hour it was;
Nothing undone
Remained; the early seeds
All safely sown.

And now, hark at the rain,
Windless and light,
Half a kiss, half a tear,
Saying good-night.

EDWARD THOMAS (1878—1917)

GREEN RAIN

Into the scented woods we'll go
And see the blackthorn swim in snow.
High above, in the budding leaves,
A brooding dove awakes and grieves;
The glades with mingled music stir,
And wildly laughs the woodpecker.
When blackthorn petals pearl the breeze,
There are the twisted hawthorn trees
Thick-set with buds, as clear and pale
As golden water or green hail—
As if a storm of rain had stood
Enchanted in the thorny wood,
And, hearing fairy voices call,
Hung poised, forgetting how to fall.

MARY WEBB (1881—1927)

In a thorn hedge at the bottom of the orchard a pair of long-tailed tits are building their nest, and every day we take them a contribution for its lining, generally plucked from the small Lakeland terrier, who is moulting now and very glad to be relieved of some of his shagginess. Mrs Tit is quite unconcerned by our visits, and when I laid an offering at her door this morning she hopped down a twig or two and looked it over, not, I felt, very appreciatively. 'What! Dog again?' her expression seemed to say as she jerked her absurd little face round towards where I stood in the lea of a lilac bush, for all the world like so many grey and black jokes hopping about in the hedges and desperately busy over some secret preparation for April Fools' Day.

'Julian', from *50 Faggots* (1944)

There are no days in the whole round year more delicious than those which often come to us in the latter half of April. On these days one goes forth in the morning, and finds an Italian warmth brooding over all the hills, taking visible shape in a glistening mist of silvered azure, with which mingles the smoke from many bonfires. The sun trembles in his own soft rays, till one understands the old English tradition, that he dances on Easter-Day. Swimming in a sea of glory, the tops of the hills look nearer than their bases, and their glistening watercourses seem close to the eye, as is their liberated murmur to the ear. All across this broad intervale the teams are ploughing. The grass in the meadow seems all to have grown green since yesterday. The blackbirds jangle in the oak, the robin is perched upon the elm, the song-sparrow on the hazel, and the bluebird on the apple-tree.

Thomas Wentworth Higginson (1823–1911),
from *In a Fair Country*, 1889

from PIPPA PASSES

The year's at the spring
 And day's at the morn;
Morning's at seven;
The hillside's dew-pearled;
The lark's on the wing;
The snail's on the thorn:
God's in His heaven—
All's right with the world!

Robert Browning (1812–1889)

SPRING TRADITIONAL COUNTRY WISDOM

The rule in gardening never forget,
To sow dry and plant wet.

One year's seeding means seven years' weeding.

A mackerel sky,
Never holds three days dry.

Ducks won't lay till they've sipped March water.

If you run after two hares, you'll catch neither.

Birds fly high, clear blue sky.
If birds fly low, then rain we shall know.

Kill not the goose that lays the golden eggs.

A swarm of bees in May
Is worth a load of hay;
A swarm of bees in June
Is worth a silver spoon;
A swarm in July,
Is not worth a fly.

When apple-trees bloom well in May,
You can eat apples night and day.

A dry May and a leaking June
Makes the farmer whistle a merry tune.

Easter Eve

I awoke at 4.30 and there was a glorious sight in the sky, one of the grand spectacles of the Universe. There was not a cloud in the deep wonderful blue of the heavens. Along the Eastern horizon there was a clear deep intense glow neither scarlet nor crimson but a mixture of both. This red glow was very narrow, almost like a riband and it suddenly shaded off into the deep blue. Opposite in the west the full moon shining in all its brilliance was setting upon the hill beyond the church steeple. Thus the glow in the east bathed the church in a warm rich tinted light, while the moon from the west was casting strong shadows. The moon dropped quickly down behind the hill bright to the last, till only her rim could be seen sparkling among the tops of the orchards on the hill. The sun rose quickly and the rays struck red upon the white walls of Penllan, but not so brilliantly as in the winter sunrisings. I got up soon after 5 and set to work on my Easter sermon getting two hours for writing before breakfast.

At 11 I went to school. Next I went to Cae Mawr. Mrs. Morrell had been very busy all the morning preparing decorations for the Font, a round dish full of flowers in water and just big enough to fit into the Font and upon this large dish a pot filled and covered with flowers all wild, primroses, violets, wood anemones, wood sorrel, periwinkles, oxlips and the first blue bells, rising in a gentle pyramid, ferns and larch sprays drooping over the brim, a wreath of simple ivy to go round the stem of the Font, and a bed of moss to encircle the foot of the Font in a narrow band pointed at the corners and angles of the stone with knots of primroses.

The Reverend Francis Kilvert (1840–1879), 16 April 1870

SPRING

Country Contentments

Glinting green shoots emerging
from the dark earth.

Catkins dangling from bare twigs,
suggestive of their other name: 'lambs' tails'.

Pink magnolias and pale blue skies.

Early dawns filled with the chorus of the birds.

Going to a cherry blossom festival.

Daffodils and tulips in jam jars on the kitchen table.

Newly laid hens' eggs gathered in a basket.

Tiny violets turning their faces to the sun.

An evening walk through a bluebell wood.

Hawthorn blossoms scenting the air.

Foraging for wild garlic.

Sitting outside on the first warm day,
listening to the blackbird's song.

The merry gurgle of a brook after the spring thaw.

Lambs frolicking in the fields on a sunny day.

Sap rising; new life all around you.

Frothy clouds of Queen Anne's lace lining country lanes.

Sore arms and legs from unaccustomed gardening.

Rainbows after April showers.

Freshly washed linen drying in the sunshine.

Listening for the call of the cuckoo.

from THE QUESTION

And in the warm hedge grew lush eglantine,
Green cowbind and the moonlight-coloured may,
And cherry-blossoms, and white cups, whose wine
Was the bright dew, yet drained not by the day;
And wild roses, and ivy serpentine,
With its dark buds and leaves, wandering astray;
And flowers azure, black, and streaked with gold,
Fairer than any wakened eyes behold.

PERCY BYSSHE SHELLEY (1792–1822)

SPRING GOETH ALL IN WHITE

Spring goeth all in white,
Crowned with milk-white may:
In fleecy flocks of light
O'er heaven the white clouds stray:

White butterflies in the air;
White daisies prank the ground:
The cherry and hoary pear
Scatter their snow around.

ROBERT BRIDGES (1844—1930)

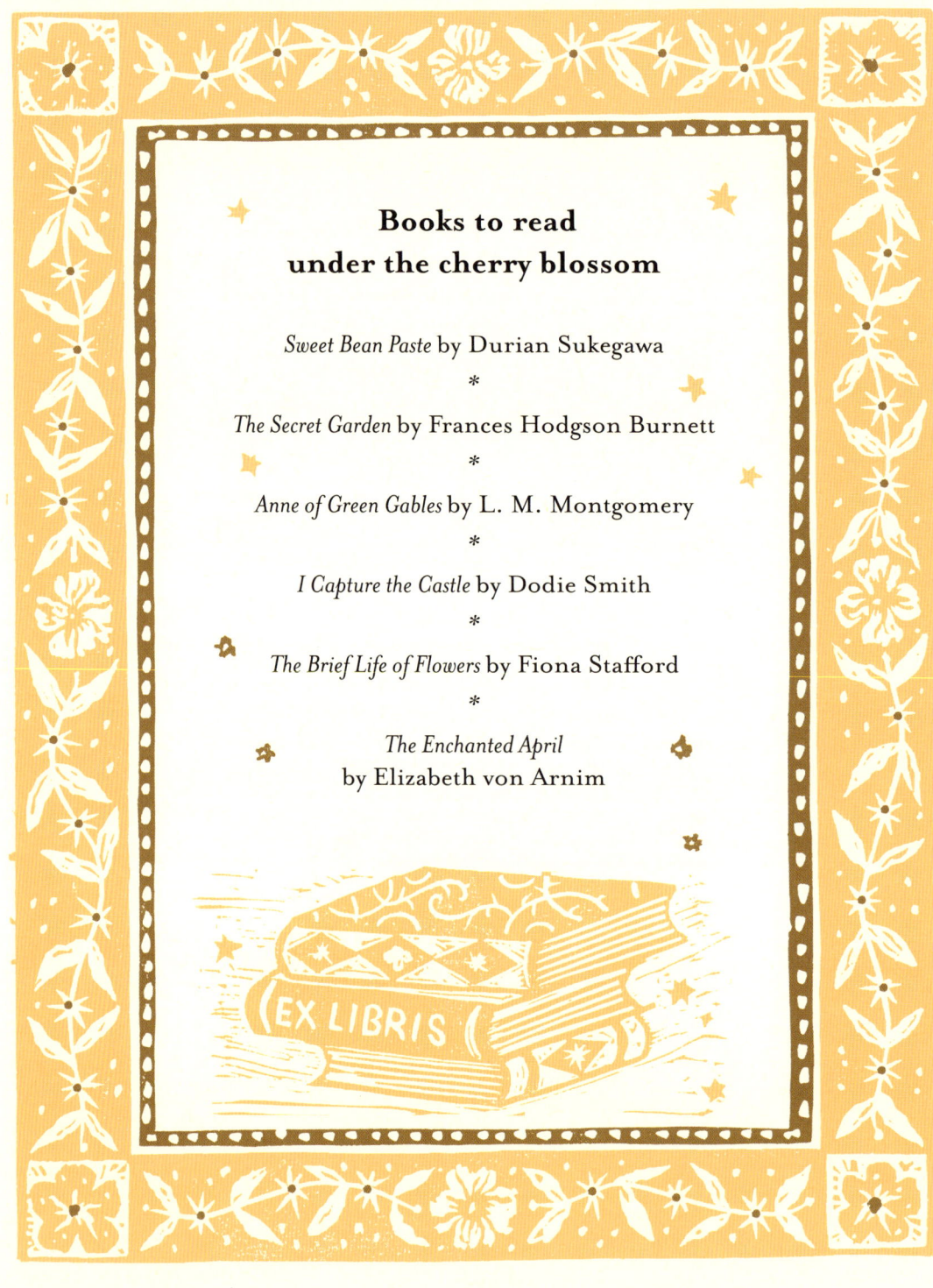

Books to read under the cherry blossom

Sweet Bean Paste by Durian Sukegawa

*

The Secret Garden by Frances Hodgson Burnett

*

Anne of Green Gables by L. M. Montgomery

*

I Capture the Castle by Dodie Smith

*

The Brief Life of Flowers by Fiona Stafford

*

The Enchanted April by Elizabeth von Arnim

from APRIL

Of all the months that fill the year
Give April's month to me,
For earth and sky are then so fill'd
With sweet variety.

The apple-blossoms' shower of rose,
The pear-tree's pearly hue,
As beautiful as woman's blush.
As evanescent too...

On every bough there is a bud,
In every bud a flower;
But scarcely bud or flower will last
Beyond the present hour.

Now comes a shower-cloud o'er the sky,
Then all again sunshine;
Then clouds again, but brighten'd with
The rainbow's color'd line.

Ay, this, this is the month for me!
I could not love a scene
Where the blue sky was always blue,
The green earth always green.

LETITIA E. LANDON (1802—1838)

from SPRING

Nothing is so beautiful as Spring –
   When weeds, in wheels, shoot long and lovely and lush;
   Thrush's eggs look little low heavens, and thrush
Through the echoing timber does so rinse and wring
The ear, it strikes like lightnings to hear him sing;
   The glassy peartree leaves and blooms, they brush
   The descending blue; that blue is all in a rush
With richness; the racing lambs too have fair their fling.

GERARD MANLEY HOPKINS (1844—1889)

Walking in a country churchyard it is often hard to think of it as a place of death. The children play among the tombs. At Easter the village girls bring hither primroses from the woods, planting some, scattering others. Labourers meet and talk there, for the footpaths all converge towards the church. Lovers walk there. The gravedigger is indeed often busy there, but you may go many times and not find him at a grave, and it is seldom but he is planting flowers, pruning bushes, or mowing grass. On the tombs themselves, in epitaph or in lack of epitaph, is written the corporate wisdom of the village, its philosophy and its history half transmuted into poetry.

Edward Thomas (1878–1917), from *The Heart of England*, 1906

Cowslips filled the rolling rich meadow called Greeny Croft, a field whose hedges were splendid with coronets of honeysuckle and masses of wild roses at mowing time. We picked the cowslips, filling the big clothes-basket, ready for cowslip wine. The scent of the flowers stirred my heart as I knelt among them and broke the brittle stalks, which snapped so readily in my fingers. The colour was richer than sunshine, as they swung their golden heads in the spring breezes, and their scent was sweeter than the rose. I sucked the flowerets of cowslip, clover and honeysuckle, to get the morsel of honey which lay within, and I nibbled the juicy stems of peeled briars.

Alison Uttley (1884–1976), from *Ambush of Young Days*, 1937

NOW LINNET

Now linnet, finch and willow-wren,
Their quilted nests must fill again,
And buds must tie their new green bows
On thin twigs where the sharp thorn grows,
And in its cradle sleeps the rose.

Now young winds spiral down the shell
Of distance where the hills of Mourne
Beyond the reaches of the Lough
Have pursued their lips into a horn.

Now cuckoo's egg in strange nest lies,
Small leaves sprout wings, and little flies
Float by on rainbow petals. Skies
Grow tender as they hear the lark
Strip one by one the scales of dark.

FREDA LAUGHTON (1907–1995)

NAMES OF COUNTRY ANIMALS AND THEIR YOUNG

ANIMAL	FEMALE	MALE	YOUNG
Badger	Sow	Boar	Cub
Cattle	Cow, Heifer	Bull, Ox, Steer	Calf
Deer	Doe, Hind	Buck, Stag	Faun
Donkey	Jenny, Jennet	Jack, Jackass	Foal
Fox	Vixen	Dog	Cub
Goat	Nanny	Billy	Kid
Goose	Goose	Gander	Gosling
Hare	Doe, Jill	Buck, Jack	Leveret
Hedgehog	Sow	Boar	Hoglet
Otter	Sow	Boar	Pup, Kits, Kittens
Pig	Sow	Boar	Piglet
Rabbit	Doe	Buck	Kit, Kitten
Sheep	Ewe	Ram	Lamb
Squirrel	Doe	Buck	Pup
Swan	Pen	Cob	Cygnet
Turkey	Hen	Tom	Poult
Weasel	Jill	Jack	Kit

WILD GARLIC & THREE CHEESE SCONES

These tasty scones can be served warm from the oven and make perfect pre-dinner nibbles with a glass of white wine on a spring evening.

Makes 16 small scones

INGREDIENTS

A small handful of freshly gathered wild garlic leaves, wiped with a damp cloth and dried gently with a clean tea towel

175g (6oz) self-raising flour, sifted

Pinch of salt

¼ tsp smoked paprika

Pinch of cayenne pepper

¼ tsp freshly ground black pepper

35g (1¼oz) chilled butter, cut into small cubes

45g (1½oz) Pecorino cheese, grated

45g (1½oz) Lancaster cheese (choose one of the hard 'Tasty' variety), grated

1 large egg, beaten with 1½ tbsp whole milk

<u>To top</u>

1½ tbsp whole milk

3 tbsp finely grated Parmesan

METHOD

1. Preheat the oven to 200°C (180°C Fan), 400°F, Gas Mark 6.
2. Cover a large baking tray with baking parchment.
3. Place the wild garlic in a mug and snip with scissors until the leaves are finely chopped.
4. Place the sifted self-raising flour, salt, smoked paprika, cayenne pepper and black pepper into a food processor. Add the cubes of chilled butter and process until well mixed.
5. Add the grated Pecorino and Lancaster cheeses, as well as the chopped wild garlic, and pulse to combine. With the food processor running, pour in the beaten egg and milk, combining until the mixture begins to clump together.
6. Turn the mixture onto a lightly floured surface and knead gently with your hands until smooth. Then pat into a round.
7. Using a rolling pin, roll out the dough to 2cm (¾ inch) thick. Using a 3cm (1 inch) round cutter, cut out as many rounds as possible – press the cutter straight down and avoid twisting it at all. Place the rounds in rows on the baking sheet as you go. Bring together any scraps and cut out more rounds, until all the dough has been used, and the rounds are all on the baking tray.
8. Lightly brush the rounds with milk and sprinkle the finely grated Parmesan on top of each scone.
9. Place in preheated oven and cook for 8–10 minutes, or until well risen and golden (but not browned on the top).
10. Transfer to a wire rack and leave to cool for a few minutes, then serve immediately.

from THE BLUEBELL

The bluebell is the sweetest flower
That waves in summer air:
Its blossoms have the mightiest power
To soothe my spirit's care.

                EMILY BRONTË (1818–1848)

Never, she thought, had the garden looked more beautiful, the lawns like velvet, the wide borders gay with every sweet old flower — columbines and Canterbury bells, lupins and sweet-williams, pansies and peonies. A chestnut grew at one side of the lawn, holding up hundreds of waxen blossoms, like some great decorated Christmas-tree. Behind, the hillside rose steeply, and a group of tall dark pines threw up effectively the white-washed house.

> O. Douglas, pseudonym of Anna Masterton Buchan (1877–1948), from *Pink Sugar*, 1928

On some very specially divine days, like today, I have actually longed for some one else to be here to enjoy the beauty with me. There has been rain in the night, and the whole garden seems to be singing — not the untiring birds only, but the vigorous plants, the happy grass and trees, the lilac bushes — oh, those lilac bushes! They are all out to-day, and the garden is drenched with the scent. I have brought in armfuls, the picking is such a delight, and every pot and bowl and tub in the house is filled with purple glory… and I long more and more for a kindred spirit — it seems so greedy to have so much loveliness to oneself — but kindred spirits are so very, very rare; I might almost as well cry for the moon. It is true that my garden is full of friends, only they are — dumb.

> Elizabeth von Arnim (1866–1941), from *Elizabeth and Her German Garden*, 1898

'For my own part,' said he, 'I am excessively fond of a cottage; there is always so much comfort, so much elegance about them. And I protest, if I had any money to spare, I should buy a little land and build one myself, within a short distance of London, where I might drive myself down at any time, and collect a few friends about me, and be happy. I advise every body who is going to build, to build a cottage. My friend Lord Courtland came to me the other day on purpose to ask my advice, and laid before me three different plans of Bonomi's. I was to decide on the best of them. "My dear Courtland," said I, immediately throwing them all into the fire, "do not adopt either of them, but by all means build a cottage." And that I fancy, will be the end of it.

'Some people imagine that there can be no accommodations, no space in a cottage; but this is all a mistake. I was last month at my friend Elliott's, near Dartford. Lady Elliott wished to give a dance. "But how can it be done?" said she; "my dear Ferrars, do tell me how it is to be managed. There is not a room in this cottage that will hold ten couple, and where can the supper be?" I immediately saw that there could be no difficulty in it, so I said, "My dear Lady Elliott, do not be uneasy. The dining parlour will admit eighteen couple with ease; card-tables may be placed in the drawing-room; the library may be open for tea and other refreshments; and let the supper be set out in the saloon." Lady Elliott was delighted with the thought. We measured the dining-room, and found it would hold exactly eighteen couple, and the affair was arranged precisely after my plan. So that, in fact, you see, if people do but know how to set about it, every comfort may be as well enjoyed in a cottage as in the most spacious dwelling.'

Elinor agreed to it all, for she did not think he deserved the compliment of rational opposition.

Jane Austen (1775–1817), from *Sense and Sensibility*, 1811

Books for a country cottage

Sense and Sensibility by Jane Austen

*

Bird Cottage by Eva Meijer

*

The Herbal Year by Christina Hart-Davies

*

Made in England by Dorothy Hartley

*

Lark Rise to Candleford by Flora Thompson

*

Cranford by Elizabeth Gaskell

MAY DAY

A delicate fabric of bird song
  Floats in the air,
The smell of wet wild earth
  Is everywhere.

Red small leaves of the maple
  Are clenched like a hand,
Like girls at their first communion
  The pear trees stand.

Oh I must pass nothing by
  Without loving it much,
The raindrop try with my lips,
  The grass with my touch;

For how can I be sure
  I shall see again
The world on the first of May
  Shining after the rain?

              Sara Teasdale (1884–1933)

We have amethyst, and blue, and deep winy purple, and white lilacs. The double and fancy lilacs are elegant, but the ordinary country-yard lilacs are my favorite. The white lilacs are more delicate in shape and odor, and white lilacs and white narcissus in a milk-glass lacy-edge bowl are near enough heaven for me any day.

In Northern Wisconsin we used to see them growing where houses once had stood, lifting their splendor by a blackened chimney or above fallen beams. Wherever an old cabin had been a home, lilacs remembered.

Gladys Taber (1899–1980), from *Stillmeadow Seasons*, 1950

This evening being May eve I ought to have put some birch and wittan (mountain ash) over the door to keep out the 'old witch.' But I was too lazy to go out and get it. Let us hope the old witch will not come in during the night. The young witches are welcome.

The Reverend Francis Kilvert (1840–1879), 30 April 1870

Good morning, ladies and gentlemen, it is the first of May,
    And we are come to garlanding because it is new May Day,
    A bunch of flowers we have brought you, and at your door
        we stay,
    So please to give us what you can, and then we'll go away.

Traditional

The forests have departed, but some old customs of their shades remain. Many, however, linger only in a metamorphosed or disguised form. The May-Day dance, for instance, was to be discerned on the afternoon under notice, in the guise of the club revel, or 'club-walking,' as it was there called.

It was an interesting event to the younger inhabitants of Marlott, though its real interest was not observed by the participators in the ceremony. Its singularity lay less in the retention of a custom of walking in procession and dancing on each anniversary than in the members being solely women…

The banded ones were all dressed in white gowns—a gay survival from Old Style days, when cheerfulness and May-time were synonyms—days before the habit of taking long views had reduced emotions to a monotonous average. Their first exhibition of themselves was in a processional march of two and two round the parish. Ideal and real clashed slightly as the sun lit up their figures against the green hedges and creeper-laced house-fronts; for, though the whole troop wore white garments, no two whites were alike among them. Some approached pure blanching; some had a bluish pallor; some worn by the older characters (which had possibly lain by folded for many a year) inclined to a cadaverous tint, and to a Georgian style.

In addition to the distinction of a white frock, every woman and girl carried in her right hand a peeled willow wand, and in her left a bunch of white flowers. The peeling of the former, and the selection of the latter, had been an operation of personal care.

Thomas Hardy (1840–1928), from *Tess of the d'Urbervilles*, 1891

THE PRETTY PLOUGHBOY

As I was a-walking
One morning in spring
I heard a pretty ploughboy,
And so sweetly he did sing;

And as he was a-singing O
These words I heard him say,
'There's no life like the ploughboy's
In the sweet month of May.'

There's the lark in the morning
She will rise up from her nest,
And she'll mount the white air
With the dew all on her breast.

And with the pretty ploughboy O
She'll whistle and she'll sing
And at night she'll return
To her nest back again.

                              Traditional

It was a warm afternoon in May. On either side of the lane the hawthorn hedges were breaking into tiny white rosettes of blossom; in the distant woods an azure haze showed the drifts of bluebells, while here and there on the banks by the roadside clusters of pale golden primroses still lingered. Cottage gardens were gay with tulips and wallflowers, lilac and laburnum....

> Richmal Crompton (1890–1969), from *Family Roundabout*, 1948

I have a very pleasant recollection of that walk, along the hard, white, sunny road, shaded here and there with bright, green trees, and adorned with flowery banks and blossoming hedges of delicious fragrance; or through pleasant fields and lanes, all glorious in the sweet flowers, and brilliant verdure of delightful May.

> Anne Brontë (1820–1849), from *The Tenant of Wildfell Hall*, 1848

The countryside around Candleford Green was richer and more varied than that near her home. Instead of flat, arable fields, there were low, green hills, and valleys and many trees and little winding streams. Her path as postwoman led over much pasture land and she often returned with her shoes powdered yellow with buttercup pollen. The copses were full of bluebells and there were kingcups and forget-me-nots by the margins of the brooks and cowslips and pale purple milkmaids in the watermeadows. Laura seldom returned from her round without more flowers in her hand than she knew what to do with. Her bedroom looked and smelled like a garden, and she stood as many pots and vases about the kitchen as Zillah would permit.

> Flora Thompson (1876–1947), from *Candleford Green*, 1943

THE CUCKOO

O the cuckoo she's a pretty bird,
She singeth as she flies,
She bringeth good tidings,
She telleth no lies.

She sucketh white flowers,
For to keep her voice clear,
And the more she singeth cuckoo,
The summer draweth near.

                              TRADITIONAL

I love tulips better than any other spring flower; they are the embodiment of alert cheerfulness and tidy grace, and next to a hyacinth look like a wholesome, freshly tubbed young girl beside a stout lady whose every movement weighs down the air with patchouli. Their faint, delicate scent is refinement itself; and is there anything in the world more charming than the sprightly way they hold up their little faces to the sun. I have heard them called bold and flaunting, but to me they seem modest grace itself, only always on the alert to enjoy life as much as they can and not afraid of looking the sun or anything else above them in the face.

Elizabeth von Arnim (1866–1941),
from Elizabeth and Her German Garden, 1898

It is not spring until you can plant your foot upon twelve daisies.

Traditional

Mr. Howes and Wife and Mrs. Davy, Mr. Bodham and his Brother, and Mr. du Quesne all dined and spent the afternoon and part of the evening with us to-day. I gave them for dinner a dish of Maccarel, 3 young Chicken boiled and some Bacon, a neck of Pork rosted and a Gooseberry Pye hot. We laughed immoderately after dinner on Mrs. Howes's being sent to Coventry by us for an Hour. What with laughing and eating hot Gooseberry Pye brought on me the Hickupps with a violent pain in my stomach which lasted till I went to bed. At Cards Quadrille this evening — lost 0.2.6.

James Woodforde (1740–1803), 18 May 1779

Gooseberry-fool. — Put the picked fruit and a glass of water into a jar with a little moist sugar, and set the jar over a stove, or in boiling water, till the fruit will pulp. Press it through a colander, and mix the pulp by degrees with cream or with common plain custard.

> Margaret Dods, pseudonym of Christian Isobel Johnstone (1781–1857), from *The Cook and Housewife's Manual*, 1826

The sun shone brightly on little showers of buttercup down the bank, in the fields the fool's-parsley was foamy, held very high and proud above a number of flowers that flitted in the greenish twilight of the mowing-grass below.

> D. H. Lawrence (1885–1930), from *The Rainbow*, 1915

Bevis… rolled over on his back on the grass, looking up at the sky. The buttercups rose high above his head, the wind blew and cooled his heated forehead, and a humble-bee hummed along: borne by the breeze from the grass there came the sweet scent of green things growing in the sunshine. Far up he saw the swallows climbing in the air; they climbed a good way almost straight up, and then suddenly came slanting down again.

> Richard Jefferies (1848–1887), from *Bevis*, 1882

THE THRUSH'S NEST

Within a thick and spreading hawthorn bush
That overhung a molehill large and round,
I heard from morn to morn a merry thrush
Sing hymns to sunrise, and I drank the sound
With joy; and often, an intruding guest,
I watched her secret toil from day to day —
How true she warped the moss to form a nest,
And modelled it within with wood and clay;
And by and by, like heath-bells gilt with dew,
There lay her shining eggs, as bright as flowers,
Ink-spotted over shells of greeny blue;
And there I witnessed, in the sunny hours,
A brood of nature's minstrels chirp and fly,
Glad as the sunshine and the laughing sky.

JOHN CLARE (1793—1864)

SILENT NOON

Your hands lie open in the long fresh grass, —
The finger-points look through like rosy blooms:
Your eyes smile peace. The pasture gleams and glooms
'Neath billowing skies that scatter and amass.
All round our nest, far as the eye can pass,
Are golden kingcup-fields with silver edge
Where the cow-parsley skirts the hawthorn-hedge.
'Tis visible silence, still as the hour-glass.
Deep in the sun-search'd growths the dragon-fly
Hangs like a blue thread loosen'd from the sky:—
So this wing'd hour is dropt to us from above.
Oh! clasp we to our hearts, for deathless dower,
This close-companion'd inarticulate hour
When twofold silence was the song of love.

DANTE GABRIEL ROSSETTI (1828—1882)

2
SUMMER

from THE SWALLOW

The swallow twitters about the eaves;
Blithely she sings, and sweet and clear;
Around her climb the woodbine leaves
In a golden atmosphere.

The summer wind sways leaf and spray,
That catch and cling to the cool gray wall;
The bright sea stretches miles away,
And the noon sun shines o'er all.

In the chamber's shadow, quietly,
I stand and worship the sky and the leaves,
The golden air and the brilliant sea,
The swallow at the eaves.

Like a living jewel she sits and sings;
Fain would I read her riddle aright,
Fain would I know whence her rapture springs,
So strong in a thing so slight!

Celia Thaxter (1835–1894)

from BACCHANALIA

The evening comes, the fields are still.
The tinkle of the thirsty rill,
Unheard all day, ascends again;
Deserted is the half-mown plain,
Silent the swaths! the ringing wain,
The mower's cry, the dog's alarms,
All housed within the sleeping farms!
The business of the day is done,
The last-left haymaker is gone.
And from the thyme upon the height,
And from the elder-blossom white
And pale dog-roses in the hedge,
And from the mint-plant in the sedge,
In puffs of balm the night-air blows
The perfume which the day forgoes.
And on the pure horizon far,
See, pulsing with the first-born star,
The liquid sky above the hill!
The evening comes, the fields are still.

Matthew Arnold (1822–1888)

FIRE-FLIES

See the air filling near by and afar,—
A shadowy host—how brilliant they are!

Silently flitting, spark upon spark,
Gemming the willows out in the dark;

Waking the night in a twinkling surprise,
Making the star-light pale where they rise;

Snowing soft fire-flakes into the grass,
Lighting the face of each daisy they pass;

Startling the darkness, over and over,
Where the sly pimpernel kisses the clover;

Piercing the duskiest heights of the pines;
Drowsily poised on the low-swinging vines;

Suddenly shifting their tapers around,
Now on the fences, and now on the ground,

Now in the bushes and tree-tops, and then
Pitching them far into darkness again;

There like a shooting-star, slowly on wing,
Here like the flash of a dowager's ring;

Setting the dark, croaking hollows a-gleam,
Spangling the gloom of the ghoul-haunted
  stream;

They pulse and they sparkle in shadowy play,
Like a night fallen down with its stars all
  astray;

They pulse and they flicker, they kindle afar,
A vanishing host,—but how brilliant they are!

        MARY MAPES DODGE (1831–1905)

It was a beautiful summer afternoon, at that delicious period of the year when summer has just burst forth from the growth of spring; when the summer is yet but three days old, and all the various shades of green which nature can put forth are still in their unsoiled purity of freshness. The apple blossoms were on the trees, and the hedges were sweet with May. The cuckoo at five o'clock was still sounding his soft summer call with unabated energy, and even the common grasses of the hedgerows were sweet with the fragrance of their new growth. The foliage of the oaks was complete, so that every bough and twig was clothed; but the leaves did not yet hang heavy in masses, and the bend of every bough and the tapering curve of every twig were visible through light green covering. There is no time of the year equal in beauty to the first week of summer: and no colour which nature gives, not even the gorgeous hues of autumn, which can equal the verdure produced by the first warm suns of May.

Anthony Trollope (1815–1882), from *Framley Parsonage*, 1861

There had never been such a June in Eagle County. Usually it was a month of moods, with abrupt alternations of belated frost and mid-summer heat; this year, day followed day in a sequence of temperate beauty. Every morning a breeze blew steadily from the hills. Toward noon it built up great canopies of white cloud that threw a cool shadow over fields and woods; then before sunset the clouds dissolved again, and the western light rained its unobstructed brightness on the valley.

On such an afternoon Charity Royall lay on a ridge above a sunlit hollow, her face pressed to the earth and the warm currents of the grass running through her. Directly in her line of vision a blackberry branch laid its frail white flowers and blue-green leaves against the sky. Just beyond, a tuft of sweet-fern uncurled between the beaded shoots of the grass, and a small yellow butterfly vibrated over them like a fleck of sunshine. This was all she saw; but she felt, above her and about her, the strong growth of the beeches clothing the ridge, the rounding of pale green cones on countless spruce-branches, the push of myriads of sweet-fern fronds in the cracks of the stony slope below the wood, and the crowding shoots of meadowsweet and yellow flags in the pasture beyond. All this bubbling of sap and slipping of sheaths and bursting of calyxes was carried to her on mingled currents of fragrance. Every leaf and bud and blade seemed to contribute its exhalation to the pervading sweetness in which the pungency of pine-sap prevailed over the spice of thyme and the subtle perfume of fern, and all were merged in a moist earth-smell that was like the breath of some huge sun-warmed animal.

Edith Wharton (1862–1937), from *Summer*, 1917

It was a perfect spot for the middle period of a Sunday in June, and its felicity seemed to come partly from an antique sun-dial which, rising in front of us and forming the centre of a small intricate parterre, measured the moments ever so slowly and made them safe for leisure and talk. The garden bloomed in the suffused afternoon, the tall beeches stood still for an example, and, behind and above us, a rose-tree of many seasons, clinging to the faded grain of the brick, expressed the whole character of the scene in a familiar exquisite smell.

Henry James (1843–1916), from *The Author of Beltraffio*, 1884

What is one to say about June—the time of perfect young summer, the fulfilment of the promise of the earlier months, and with as yet no sign to remind one that its fresh young beauty will ever fade? For my own part I wander up into the wood and say, 'June is here—June is here; thank God for lovely June!' The soft cooing of the wood-dove, the glad song of many birds, the flitting of butterflies, the hum of all the little winged people among the branches, the sweet earth-scents—all seem to say the same, with an endless reiteration, never wearying because so gladsome. It is the offering of the Hymn of Praise! The lizards run in and out of the heathy tufts in the hot sunshine, and as the long day darkens the night-jar trolls out his strange song, so welcome because it is the prelude to the perfect summer night; here and there a glowworm shows its little lamp. June is here—June is here; thank God for lovely June!

And June is the time of Roses. I have great delight in the best of the old garden Roses; the Provence (Cabbage Rose), sweetest of all sweets, and the Moss Rose, its crested variety; the early Damask, and its red and white striped kind; the old, nearly single, Reine Blanche. I do not know the origin of this charming Rose, but by its appearance it should be related to the Damask. A good many years ago I came upon it in a cottage garden in Sussex, and thought I had found a white Damask. The white is a creamy white, the outsides of the outer petals are stained with red, first showing clearly in the bud. The scent is delicate and delightful, with a faint suspicion of Magnolia.

Gertrude Jekyll (1843–1932), from *Wood and Garden*, 1899

from A NIGHT IN JUNE

The sun has long been set,
The stars are out by twos and threes,
The little birds are piping yet
Among the bushes and trees;
There's a cuckoo, and one or two thrushes,
And a far-off wind that rushes,
And a sound of water that gushes,
And the cuckoo's sovereign cry
Fills all the hollow of the sky.

    William Wordsworth (1770–1850)

SWIFT

I saw swifts today, a small ashy vortex
turning scarf in the maghrib sky, and I remembered
the poet in Ledbury who told me they were

African visitors here for the summer. I thought
of my grandmother, but not with her wings jammed
against the back of a floral chair in a tiny box,

instead a swift with scythelike wings curved
Skywards in her burgundy jilbab, eyelashes flooded
with rain prayer, her hair soft patches of henna like

copper burning through streams. All those mid-flight
duas that never land. Now, I watch the flight
of aunties whirling through living rooms, arguing

over this last winter, the cost of oak, never giving
the daughters-in-law her gold bangles, and how
the war turned their summers here into a lifetime.

Warda Yassin

from AMONG THE HILLS

A single hay-cart down the dusty road
Creaks slowly, with its driver fast asleep
On the load's top. Against the neighboring hill,
Huddled along the stone wall's shady side,
The sheep show white, as if a snowdrift still
Defied the dog-star. Through the open door
A drowsy smell of flowers — gay heliotrope,
And white sweet clover, and shy mignonette —
Comes faintly in, and silent chorus lends
To the pervading symphony of peace.

JOHN GREENLEAF WHITTIER
(1807—1892)

Tuesday, 19th June.–Fine strawberries from the fields this evening for tea. Warm, bright weather; thermometer 85–lovely evening, but too warm for much exercise. Strolled in the lane, enjoying the fragrant meadows, and the waving corn-fields on the skirts of the village.

A meadow near at hand would seem to give more pleasure than a corn-field. Grain, to appear to full advantage, should be seen at a little distance, where one may note the changes in its coloring with the advancing season, where one may enjoy the play of light when the summer clouds throw their shadows there, or the breezes chase one another over the waving lawn. It is like a piece of shaded silk which the salesman throws off a little, that you may better appreciate the effect. But a meadow is a delicate embroidery in colors, which you must examine closely to understand all its merits; the nearer you are, the better. One must bend over the grass to find the blue violet in May, the red strawberry in June; one should be close at hand to mark the first appearance of the simple field-blossoms, clover, red and white, buttercup and daisy, with the later lily, and primrose, and meadow-tuft; one should be nigh to breathe the sweet and fresh perfume, which increases daily until the mowers come with their scythes.

Susan Fenimore Cooper (1813–1894), from *Rural Hours*, 1850

Mrs. Elton, in all her apparatus of happiness, her large bonnet and her basket, was very ready to lead the way in gathering, accepting, or talking—strawberries, and only strawberries, could now be thought or spoken of.— "The best fruit in England—every body's favourite—always wholesome.—These the finest beds and finest sorts.—Delightful to gather for one's self—the only way of really enjoying them.—Morning decidedly the best time—never tired—every sort good—hautboy infinitely superior—no comparison—the others hardly eatable—hautboys very scarce—Chili preferred—white wood finest flavour of all—price of strawberries in London—abundance about Bristol—Maple Grove—cultivation—beds when to be renewed—gardeners thinking exactly different—no general rule—gardeners never to be put out of their way—delicious fruit—only too rich to be eaten much of—inferior to cherries—currants more refreshing—only objection to gathering strawberries the stooping—glaring sun—tired to death—could bear it no longer—must go and sit in the shade."

Jane Austen (1775–1817), from *Emma*, 1815

The summer was hot, and the vast room cool and quiet. The time was three o'clock — immediately, that is, after luncheon. Through the narrow open windows sweet airs and scents came in from the bright world outside. Sometimes a bee would wander up from the fruit-gardens below, and lazily drone round shady corners. Sometimes a flock of pigeons rose swiftly in front of the windows, with a flash of shining wings. Every quarter of an hour the cathedral clock down in the town sent up its slow chime. Voices of people boating on the river floated up too, softened to melodiousness. Down at the foot of the hill the red roofs of the town glistened in the sun. Beyond them lay the sweltering cornfields. Beyond them forests and villages. Beyond them a blue line of hills.

Elizabeth von Arnim (1866–1941), from *Princess Priscilla's Fortnight*, 1905

from

THE OLD VICARAGE, GRANTCHESTER

Ah God! to see the branches stir
Across the moon at Grantchester!
To smell the thrilling-sweet and rotten
Unforgettable, unforgotten
River-smell, and hear the breeze
Sobbing in the little trees.
Say, do the elm-clumps greatly stand
Still guardians of that holy land?
The chestnuts shade, in reverend dream,
The yet unacademic stream?
Is dawn a secret shy and cold
Anadyomene, silver-gold?
And sunset still a golden sea
From Haslingfield to Madingley?

And after, ere the night is born,
Do hares come out about the corn?
Oh, is the water sweet and cool,
Gentle and brown, above the pool?
And laughs the immortal river still
Under the mill, under the mill?
Say, is there Beauty yet to find?
And Certainty? and Quiet kind?
Deep meadows yet, for to forget
The lies, and truths, and pain? ... oh! yet
Stands the Church clock at ten to three?
And is there honey still for tea?

RUPERT BROOKE (1887–1915)

The garden was one of those old-fashioned paradises which hardly exist any longer except as memories of our childhood: no finical separation between flower and kitchen garden there; no monotony of enjoyment for one sense to the exclusion of another; but a charming paradisiacal mingling of all that was pleasant to the eyes and good for food. The rich flower-border running along every walk, with its endless succession of spring flowers, anemones, auriculas, wall-flowers, sweet-williams, campanulas, snapdragons, and tiger-lilies, had its taller beauties, such as moss and Provence roses, varied with espalier apple-trees; the crimson of a carnation was carried out in the lurking crimson of the neighbouring strawberry-beds; you gathered a moss-rose one moment and a bunch of currants the next; you were in a delicious fluctuation between the scent of jasmine and the juice of gooseberries.

Then what a high wall at one end, flanked by a summer-house so lofty, that after ascending its long flight of steps you could see perfectly well there was no view worth looking at; what alcoves and garden-seats in all directions; and along one side, what a hedge, tall, and firm, and unbroken, like a green wall!

George Eliot (1819–1880), from *Scenes of Clerical Life*, 1858

Every fine day, throughout the summer, she sat there 'watching the bees'. She was combining duty and pleasure, for, if they swarmed, she was making sure of not losing the swarm; and, if they did not, it was still, as she said, 'a trate' to sit there, feeling the warmth of the sun, smelling the flowers, and watching 'the craturs' go in and out of the hives.

Flora Thompson (1876–1947), from *Lark Rise*, 1939

from ELEGY WRITTEN IN A COUNTRY CHURCHYARD

The curfew tolls the knell of parting day,
    The lowing herd wind slowly o'er the lea,
The plowman homeward plods his weary way,
    And leaves the world to darkness and to me.

Now fades the glimm'ring landscape on the sight,
    And all the air a solemn stillness holds,
Save where the beetle wheels his droning flight,
    And drowsy tinklings lull the distant folds;

Save that from yonder ivy-mantled tow'r
    The moping owl does to the moon complain
Of such, as wand'ring near her secret bow'r,
    Molest her ancient solitary reign.

Beneath those rugged elms, that yew-tree's shade,
    Where heaves the turf in many a mould'ring heap,
Each in his narrow cell for ever laid,
    The rude forefathers of the hamlet sleep.

The breezy call of incense-breathing Morn,
    The swallow twitt'ring from the straw-built shed,
The cock's shrill clarion, or the echoing horn,
    No more shall rouse them from their lowly bed.

                        Thomas Gray (1716–1771)

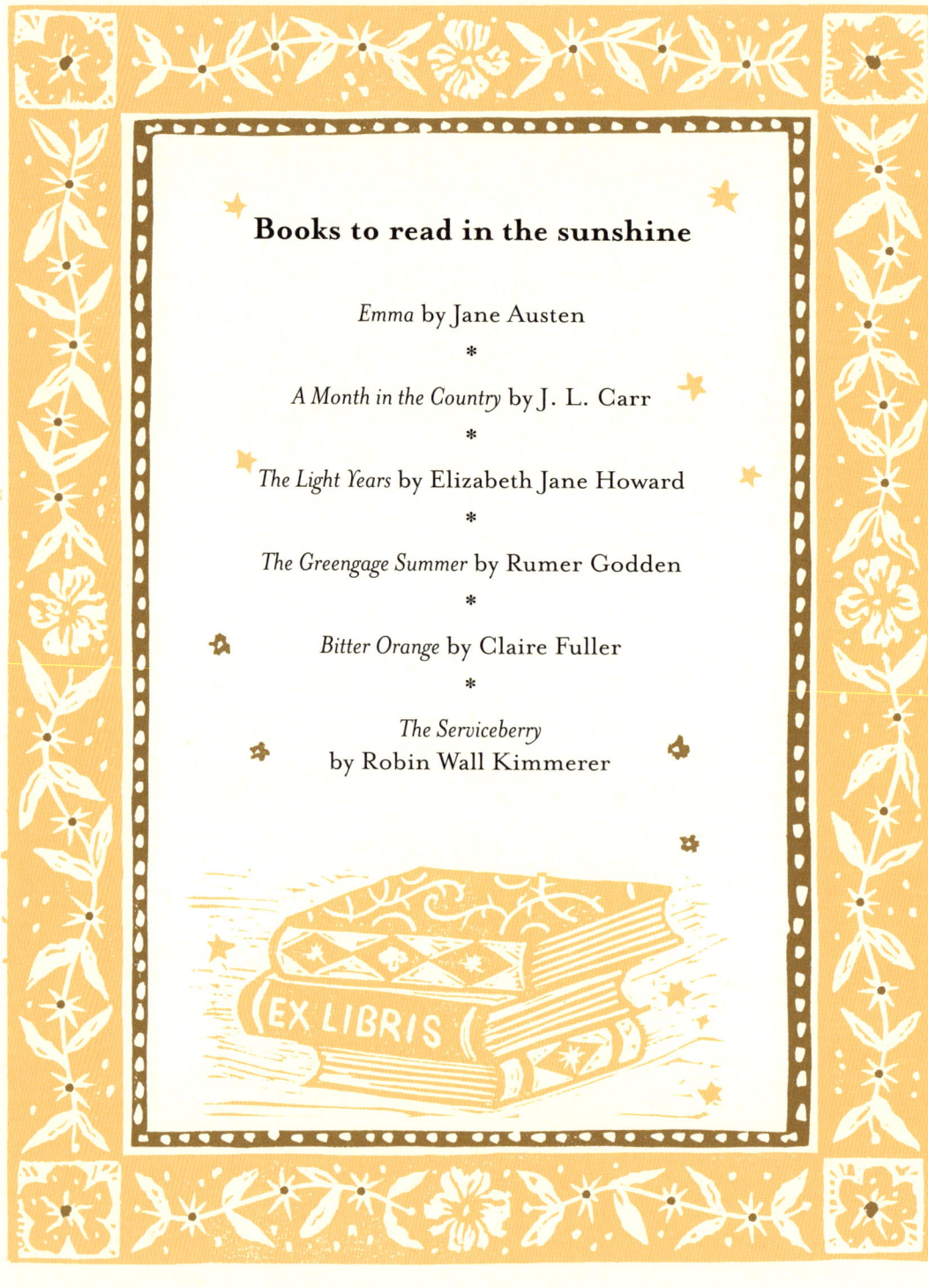

Books to read in the sunshine

Emma by Jane Austen

*

A Month in the Country by J. L. Carr

*

The Light Years by Elizabeth Jane Howard

*

The Greengage Summer by Rumer Godden

*

Bitter Orange by Claire Fuller

*

The Serviceberry by Robin Wall Kimmerer

SUMMER SHOWER

A drop fell on the apple tree,
Another on the roof;
A half a dozen kissed the eaves,
And made the gables laugh.

A few went out to help the brook,
That went to help the sea.
Myself conjectured, were they pearls,
What necklaces could be!

The dust replaced in hoisted roads,
The birds jocoser sung;
The sunshine threw his hat away,
The orchards spangles hung.

The breezes brought dejected lutes,
And bathed them in the glee;
The East put out a single flag,
And signed the fete away.

                    Emily Dickinson (1830–1886)

My Great-uncle Silas used to live in a small stone reed-thatched cottage on the edge of a pine-wood, where nightingales sang passionately in great numbers through early summer nights and on into the mornings and often still in the afternoons. On summer days after rain the air was sweetly saturated with the fragrance of the pines, which mingled subtly with the exquisite honeysuckle scent, the strange vanilla heaviness from the creamy elder-flowers in the garden hedge and the perfume of old pink and white crimped-double roses of forgotten names. It was very quiet there except for the soft, water-whispering sound of leaves and boughs, and the squabbling and singing of birds in the house-thatch and the trees. The house itself was soaked with years of scents, half-sweet, half-dimly-sour with the smell of wood smoke, the curious odour of mauve and milk-coloured and red geraniums, of old wine and tea and the earth smell of my Uncle Silas himself.

H. E. Bates (1905–1974), from *My Uncle Silas*, 1939

The seeds Dickon and Mary had planted grew as if fairies had tended them. Satiny poppies of all tints danced in the breeze by the score, gaily defying flowers which had lived in the garden for years and which it might be confessed seemed rather to wonder how such new people had got there. And the roses — the roses! Rising out of the grass, tangled round the sun-dial, wreathing the tree trunks and hanging from their branches, climbing up the walls and spreading over them with long garlands falling in cascades — they came alive day by day, hour by hour. Fair fresh leaves, and buds — and buds — tiny at first but swelling and working Magic until they burst and uncurled into cups of scent delicately spilling themselves over their brims and filling the garden air.

Frances Hodgson Burnett (1849–1924), from *The Secret Garden*, 1911

Behind these snapdragons Mme Pierre Oger, the exquisite one, the beauty, holds up her pale pink flowers. These are quite enchanting, and I feel I am watching something in a fairytale as I contemplate them. The small round cups are like the china in a doll's tea-service, or like the shell roses under the glass case in a Victorian parlour. Each petal is deeply curved, each flower is spherical, some are shaded pink and white, some rosy; others white, and they change colour with the weather. In August they will be different and again in September they will alter. On certain days they are so pale and wan with the hot sun I feel pale and wan in sympathy. They are too sad to be gathered. On other days they are radiantly happy, bright pink, eager to look around, and again they must not be picked because they are too beautiful. They seem to lose something of their perfection when they are gathered. I have had this Bourbon rose only a year, and I always visit it first thing in the morning, to find a new surprise, either in the colour or in the opening round cups.

Alison Uttley (1884–1976), from *A Year in the Country*, 1957

I am sure that I must have visited a number of vicarage gardens in my early years, for my parents were churchgoers, and my maiden aunts were stalwart helpers in Sunday schools, church bazaars and fêtes… But the vicarage garden I remember most clearly was one in Kent when I was about eight or nine. A fund-raising fête was held in dazzling sunshine. Everything proper to the occasion was there; the cake stall, the coconut shies, the bustling tea-ladies. And best of all, the penny stall, where I bought a magnificent white ostrich-feather fan which was heavily moulting, but no less enchanting. Perhaps, for me, that Edwardian relic accounts for the happiness I feel when the subject of vicarage gardens crops up, that vision of a blessed plot where it is always summer afternoon.

Miss Read (1913–2012), from *The English Vicarage Garden*, 1988

WIND ON THE CORN

Full often as I rove by path or stile,
To watch the harvest ripening in the vale,
Slowly and sweetly, like a growing smile—
A smile that ends in laughter—the quick gale
Upon the breadths of gold-green wheat descends;
While still the swallow, with unbaffled grace,
About his viewless quarry dips and bends—
And all the fine excitement of the chase
Lies in the hunter's beauty: In the eclipse
Of that brief shadow, how the barley's beard
Tilts at the passing gloom, and wild-rose dips
Among the white-tops in the ditches rear'd:
And hedgerow's flowery breast of lacework stirs
Faintly in that full wind that rocks the outstanding firs.

Charles Tennyson Turner (1808–1879)

SUMMER TRADITIONAL COUNTRY WISDOM

He that has sheep, swine and bees,
Sleep he or wake he, he may thrive.

When June brings the first dogrose,
Count eleven weeks to harvest.

A dripping June sets all in tune.

It is better to be stung by a nettle than pricked by a rose.

One straw will show which way the wind blows.

A still bee gathers no honey.

If on St Swithin's day it rain,
For forty days it will remain.

Good elm, good barley; good oak, good wheat.

It is ill prizing of green barley.

If the 24th of August be fair and clear,
Look for a prosperous autumn that year.

THE ROSE

The lily has a smooth stalk,
Will never hurt your hand;
But the rose upon her brier
Is lady of the land.

There's sweetness in an apple tree,
And profit in the corn;
But lady of all beauty
Is a rose upon a thorn.

When with moss and honey
She tips her bending brier,
And half unfolds her glowing heart,
She sets the world on fire.

CHRISTINA ROSSETTI (1830—1894)

And after all the weather was ideal. They could not have had a more perfect day for a garden-party if they had ordered it. Windless, warm, the sky without a cloud. Only the blue was veiled with a haze of light gold, as it is sometimes in early summer. The gardener had been up since dawn, mowing the lawns and sweeping them, until the grass and the dark flat rosettes where the daisy plants had been seemed to shine. As for the roses, you could not help feeling they understood that roses are the only flowers that impress people at garden-parties; the only flowers that everybody is certain of knowing. Hundreds, yes, literally hundreds, had come out in a single night; the green bushes bowed down as though they had been visited by archangels.

    Katherine Mansfield (1888–1923), from *The Garden Party*, 1922

What she liked was candy buttons, and books, and painted music (deep blue, or delicate silver) and the west sky, so altering, viewed from the steps of the back porch; and dandelions.

 She would have liked a lotus, or China asters or the Japanese Iris, or meadow lilies — yes, she would have liked meadow lilies, because the very word meadow made her breathe more deeply, and either fling her arms or want to fling her arms, depending on who was by, rapturously up to whatever was watching in the sky. But dandelions were chiefly what she saw. Yellow jewels for everyday, studding the patched green dress of her back yard. She liked the demure prettiness second to their everydayness; for in that latter quality she thought she saw a picture of herself, and it was comforting to find that what was common could also be a flower.

    Gwendolyn Brooks (1917–2000), from *Maud Martha*, 1953

Honey for Tea
Delicious Honey Varieties

Acacia blossom honey

Borage honey

Clover honey

Heather honey

Lavender honey

Orange blossom honey

Rosemary honey

Thyme honey

Manuka honey

Wildflower honey

TO A BUTTERFLY

I've watched you now a full half-hour,
Self-poised upon that yellow flower;
And, little Butterfly! indeed
I know not if you sleep or feed.
How motionless! – not frozen seas
More motionless! and then
What joy awaits you, when the breeze
Hath found you out among the trees,
And calls you forth again!

This plot of orchard-ground is ours;
My trees they are, my Sister's flowers;
Here rest your wing when they are weary;
Here lodge as in a sanctuary!
Come often to us, fear no wrong;
Sit near us on the bough!
We'll talk of sunshine and of song,
And summer days, when we were young;
Sweet childish days, that were as long
As twenty days are now.

William Wordsworth (1770–1850)

from I STOOD TIP-TOE ON A LITTLE HILL

Here are sweet peas, on tip-toe for a flight:
With wings of gentle flush o'er delicate white,
And taper fingers catching at all things,
To bind them all about with tiny rings.

John Keats (1795–1821)

There was an unaccountable strangeness about Harris. It was something more than mere ordinary tiredness. He pulled the boat against a part of the bank from which it was quite impossible for us to get into it, and immediately went to sleep. It took us an immense amount of screaming and roaring to wake him up again and put some sense into him; but we succeeded at last, and got safely on board.

Harris had a sad expression on him, so we noticed, when we got into the boat. He gave you the idea of a man who had been through trouble. We asked him if anything had happened, and he said —

'Swans!'

It seemed we had moored close to a swan's nest, and, soon after George and I had gone, the female swan came back, and kicked up a row about it. Harris had chivied her off, and she had gone away, and fetched up her old man. Harris said he had had quite a fight with these two swans; but courage and skill had prevailed in the end, and he had defeated them.

Half-an-hour afterwards they returned with eighteen other swans! It must have been a fearful battle, so far as we could understand Harris's account of it. The swans had tried to drag him and Montmorency out of the boat and drown them; and he had defended himself like a hero for four hours, and had killed the lot, and they had all paddled away to die.

'How many swans did you say there were?' asked George.

'Thirty-two,' replied Harris, sleepily.

'You said eighteen just now,' said George.

'No, I didn't,' grunted Harris; 'I said twelve. Think I can't count?'

What were the real facts about these swans we never found out. We questioned Harris on the subject in the morning, and he said, 'What swans?' and seemed to think that George and I had been dreaming.

Jerome K. Jerome (1859–1927), from *Three Men in a Boat*, 1889

SUMMER
Country Contentments

Eating peas fresh from the pod.

The drowsy hum of bumble-bees.

Newly cut grass and honeyed roses scenting the air.

Pimms with friends in the garden.

The thwack of the cricket bat.

Freshly picked strawberries and lashings of cream.

A laden picnic basket.

Visiting country gardens.

Jars of homemade jams and chutneys.

Lying on the grass and watching the aerial acrobatics of swallows in the blue sky above.

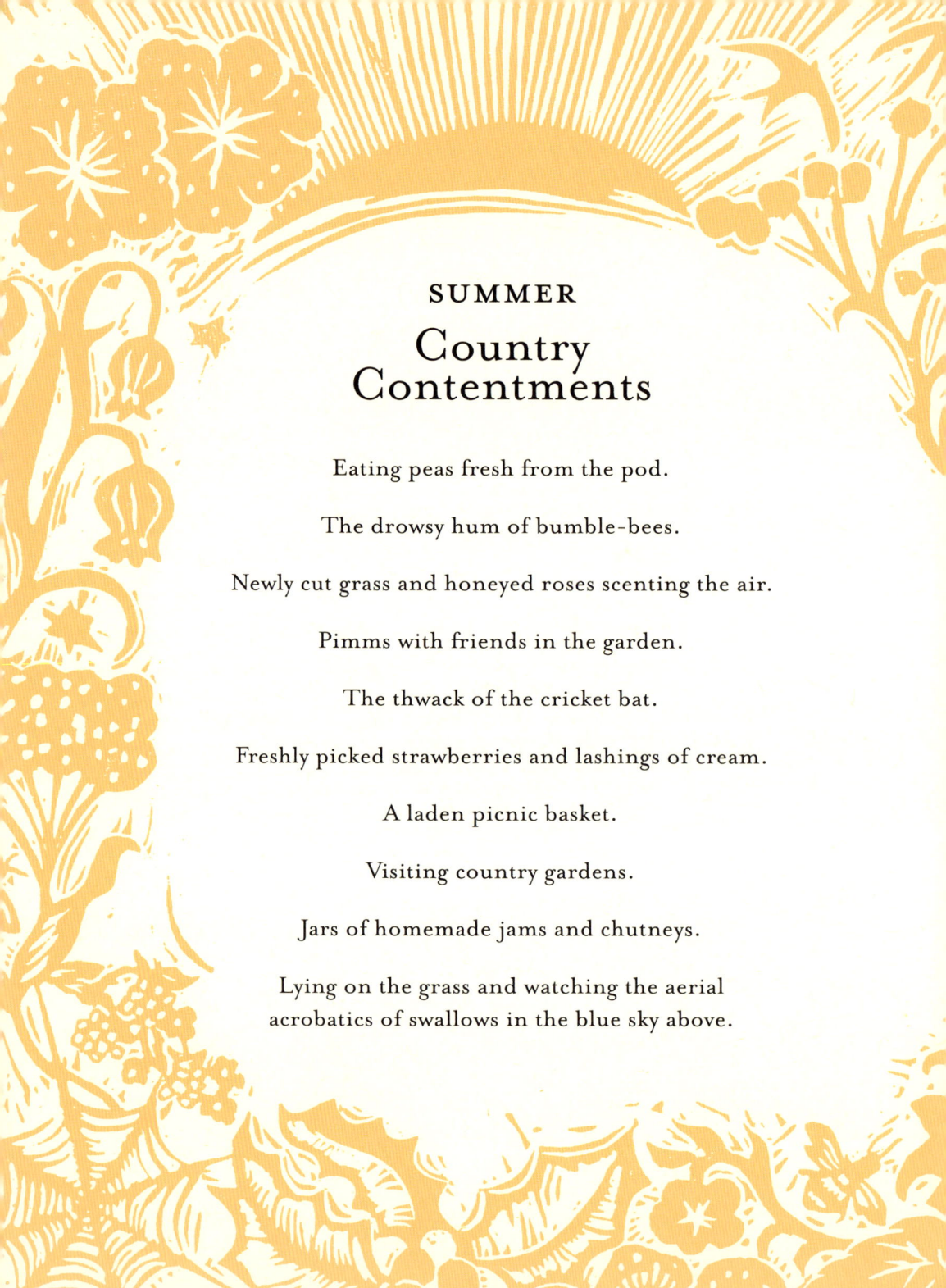

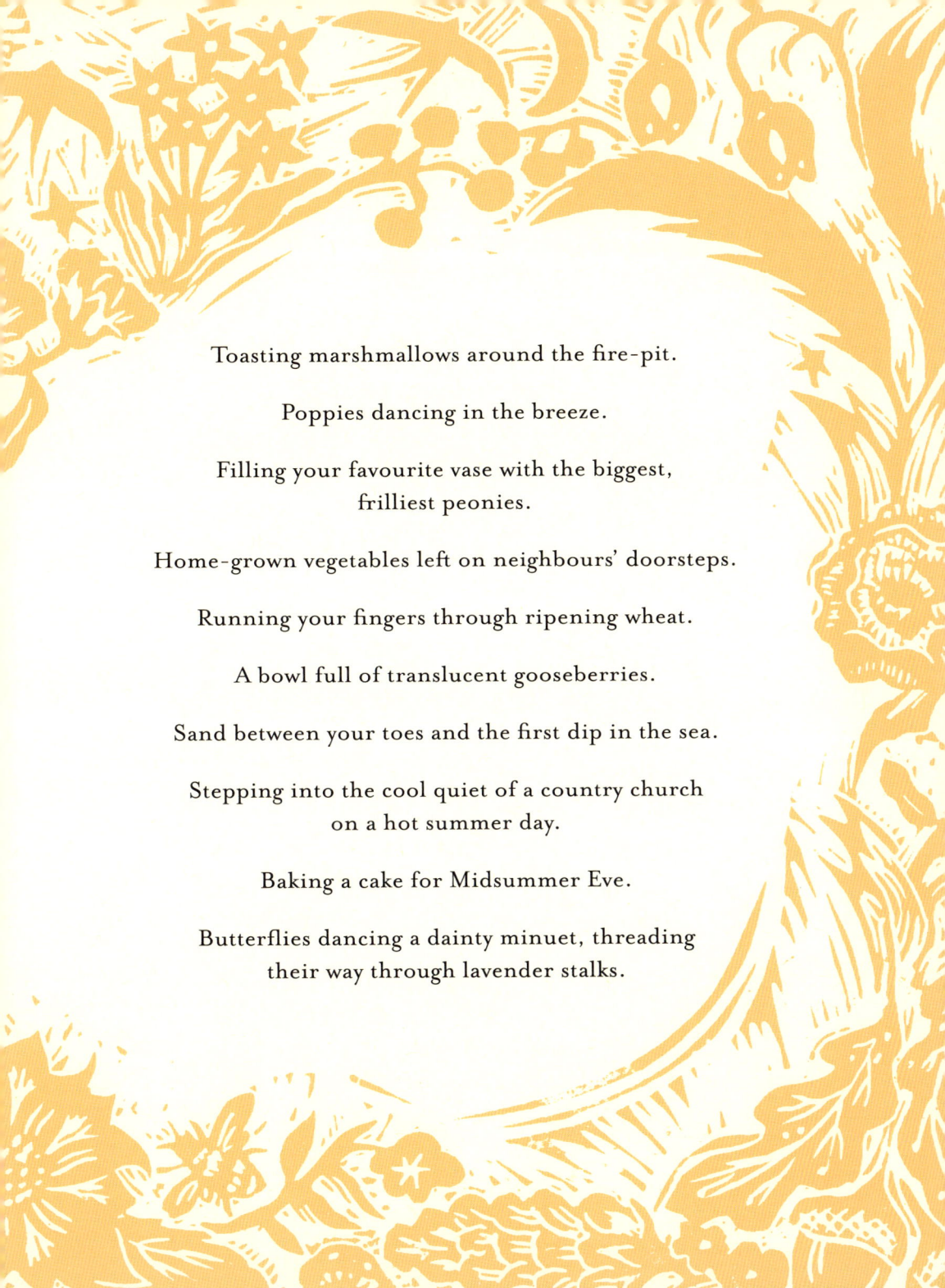

Toasting marshmallows around the fire-pit.

Poppies dancing in the breeze.

Filling your favourite vase with the biggest, frilliest peonies.

Home-grown vegetables left on neighbours' doorsteps.

Running your fingers through ripening wheat.

A bowl full of translucent gooseberries.

Sand between your toes and the first dip in the sea.

Stepping into the cool quiet of a country church on a hot summer day.

Baking a cake for Midsummer Eve.

Butterflies dancing a dainty minuet, threading their way through lavender stalks.

It is pleasant, on a sunny day to walk through a field of wheat when the footpath is bordered on either side by the ripening crop, without the intervention of hedge or fence. Such a footpath, narrow, but well kept, leads from a certain country churchyard to the highway road, and passes on the way a wicket gate in a thick evergreen shrubbery which surrounds the vicarage lawn and gardens. This afternoon the wheat stands still and upright, without a motion, in the burning sunshine, for the sun, though he has sloped a little from his highest meridian altitude, pours an even fiercer beam than at the exact hour of noon. The shadeless field is exposed to the full glare of the brilliant light. There are no trees in the field itself, the hedges are cut low and trimmed to the smallest proportions, and are devoid of timber; and, as the ground is high and close to the hills, all the trees in sight are beneath, and can be overlooked. Whether in sunshine or storm there is no shelter—no medium; the wind rushes over with its utmost fury, or the heat rests on it undisturbed by the faintest current. Yet, sultry as it is, the footpath is a pleasant one to follow.

The wheat ears, all but ripe—to the ordinary eye they are ripe, but the farmer is not quite satisfied—rise to the waist or higher, and tempt the hand to pluck them. Butterflies flutter over the surface, now descending to some flower hidden beneath, now resuming their joyous journey. There is a rich ripe feeling in the very atmosphere, the earth is yielding her wealth, and a delicate aroma rises from her generous gifts. Far as the eye can see, the rolling plains and slopes present various tints of yellow—wheat in different stages of ripeness, or of different kinds; oats and barley—till the hedges and woods of the vale conceal the farther landscape on the one hand and the ridge of the hills upon the other.

Richard Jefferies (1848–1887), from *Hodge and His Masters*, 1880

from GITANJALI

Today the summer has come at my window with its sighs and murmurs; and the bees are plying their minstrelsy at the court of the flowering grove.

        Rabindranath Tagore (1861–1941)

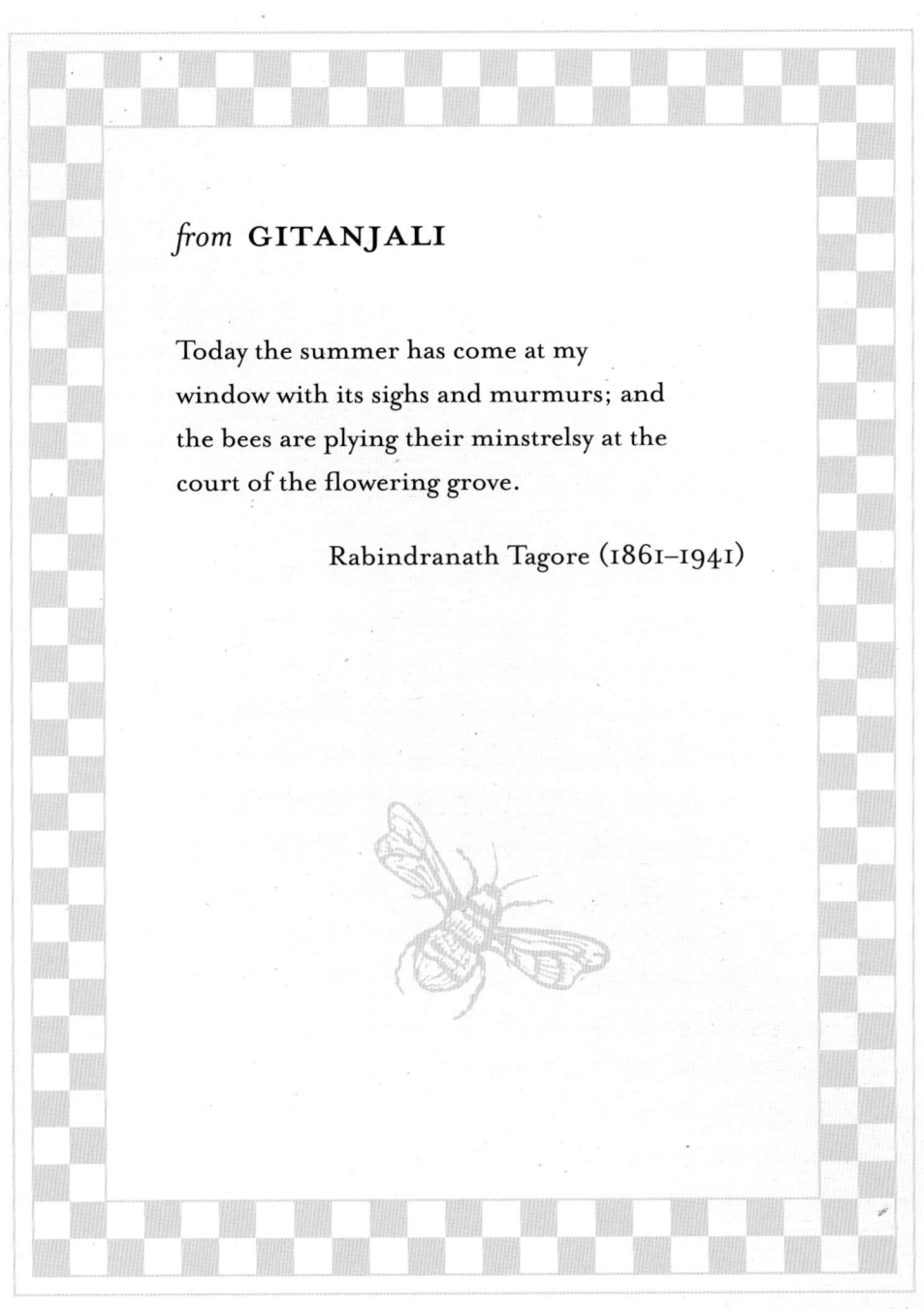

ROSES

You love the roses — so do I. I wish
The sky would rain down roses, as they rain
From off the shaken bush. Why will it not?
Then all the valley would be pink and white
And soft to tread on. They would fall as light
As feathers, smelling sweet; and it would be
Like sleeping and like waking, all at once!

GEORGE ELIOT (1819—1880)

ROSE PETAL & CINNAMON TEA

A refreshingly sweet floral tea to enjoy
on a mild summer afternoon.

To make one pot of tea

INGREDIENTS

2 heaped tbsp of good quality, dried rose petals

1 cinnamon stick, broken if necessary so that it can sit in the teapot

Honey or quince jelly, to taste

METHOD

1. Place the dried rose petals and cinnamon stick in a teapot. Pour over boiling water and stir.

2. Leave to infuse for 4 to 6 minutes, then stir again and pour through a tea strainer into your prettiest teacups.

3. Sweeten to taste with a small amount of honey or quince jelly.

4. Sit back and sip, enjoying the fragrance of this floral tea.

The Mole waggled his toes from sheer happiness, spread his chest with a sigh of full contentment, and leaned back blissfully into the soft cushions. 'What a day I'm having!' he said. 'Let us start at once!'

'Hold hard a minute, then!' said the Rat. He looped the painter through a ring in his landing-stage, climbed up into his hole above, and after a short interval reappeared staggering under a fat, wicker luncheon-basket.

'Shove that under your feet,' he observed to the Mole, as he passed it down into the boat. Then he untied the painter and took the sculls again.

'What's inside it?' asked the Mole, wriggling with curiosity.

'There's cold chicken inside it,' replied the Rat briefly; coldbeefpickledgherkinssaladfrenchrollscresssandwichespotted meatgingerbeerlemonadesodawater——'

'O stop, stop,' cried the Mole in ecstasies: 'This is too much!'

'Do you really think so?' enquired the Rat seriously. 'It's only what I always take on these little excursions; and the other animals are always telling me that I'm a mean beast and cut it very fine!'

Kenneth Grahame (1859–1932), from *The Wind in the Willows*, 1908

On Midsummer-eve, Adèle, weary with gathering wild strawberries in Hay Lane half the day, had gone to bed with the sun. I watched her drop asleep, and when I left her, I sought the garden…

I walked a while on the pavement; but a subtle, well-known scent—that of a cigar—stole from some window; I saw the library casement open a handbreadth; I knew I might be watched thence; so I went apart into the orchard. No nook in the grounds more sheltered and more Eden-like; it was full of trees, it bloomed with flowers: a very high wall shut it out from the court, on one side; on the other, a beech avenue screened it from the lawn. At the bottom was a sunk fence; its sole separation from lonely fields: a winding walk, bordered with laurels and terminating in a giant horse-chestnut, circled at the base by a seat, led down to the fence. Here one could wander unseen. While such honey-dew fell, such silence reigned, such gloaming gathered, I felt as if I could haunt such shade for ever; but in threading the flower and fruit parterres at the upper part of the enclosure, enticed there by the light the now rising moon cast on this more open quarter, my step is stayed—not by sound, not by sight, but once more by a warning fragrance.

Sweet-briar and southernwood, jasmine, pink, and rose have long been yielding their evening sacrifice of incense: this new scent is neither of shrub nor flower; it is—I know it well—it is Mr. Rochester's cigar. I look round and I listen. I see trees laden with ripening fruit. I hear a nightingale warbling in a wood half a mile off; no moving form is visible, no coming step audible; but that perfume increases: I must flee. I make for the wicket leading to the shrubbery, and I see Mr. Rochester entering. I step aside into the ivy recess; he will not stay long: he will soon return whence he came, and if I sit still he will never see me.

But no—eventide is as pleasant to him as to me, and this antique garden as attractive; and he strolls on, now lifting the gooseberry-tree branches to look at the fruit, large as plums, with which they are laden; now taking a ripe cherry from the wall; now stooping towards a knot of flowers, either to inhale their fragrance or to admire the dew-beads on their petals. A great moth goes humming by me; it alights on a plant at Mr. Rochester's foot: he sees it, and bends to examine it.

Charlotte Brontë (1816–1855), from *Jane Eyre*, 1847

Summer Wildflowers to Spot in the British Countryside

Field Poppy
Foxglove
Cornflower
Honeysuckle
Forget-me-not
Red Clover
Yellow-rattle
Herb Robert
Common Vetch
Meadow Buttercup
Dandelion

JASMINE

Plants that wake when others sleep —
Timid jasmine buds that keep
Their fragrance to themselves all day,
But when the sunlight dies away
Let the delicious secret out
To every breeze that roams about

                THOMAS MOORE (1779—1852)

THE BROOK

I come from haunts of coot and hern,
I make a sudden sally
And sparkle out among the fern,
To bicker down a valley.

By thirty hills I hurry down,
Or slip between the ridges,
By twenty thorpes, a little town,
And half a hundred bridges.

Till last by Philip's farm I flow
To join the brimming river,
For men may come and men may go,
But I go on for ever.

I chatter over stony ways,
In little sharps and trebles,
I bubble into eddying bays,
I babble on the pebbles.

With many a curve my banks I fret
By many a field and fallow,
And many a fairy foreland set
With willow-weed and mallow.

I chatter, chatter, as I flow
To join the brimming river,
For men may come and men may go,
But I go on for ever.

I wind about, and in and out,
With here a blossom sailing,
And here and there a lusty trout,
And here and there a grayling,

And here and there a foamy flake
Upon me, as I travel
With many a silvery waterbreak
Above the golden gravel,

And draw them all along, and flow
To join the brimming river
For men may come and men may go,
But I go on for ever.

I steal by lawns and grassy plots,
I slide by hazel covers;
I move the sweet forget-me-nots
That grow for happy lovers.

I slip, I slide, I gloom, I glance,
Among my skimming swallows;
I make the netted sunbeam dance
Against my sandy shallows.

I murmur under moon and stars
In brambly wildernesses;
I linger by my shingly bars;
I loiter round my cresses;

And out again I curve and flow
To join the brimming river,
For men may come and men may go,
But I go on for ever.

        Alfred, Lord Tennyson (1809–1892)

Under certain circumstances there are few hours in life more agreeable than the hour dedicated to the ceremony known as afternoon tea. There are circumstances in which, whether you partake of the tea or not—some people of course never do,—the situation is in itself delightful. Those that I have in mind in beginning to unfold this simple history offered an admirable setting to an innocent pastime. The implements of the little feast had been disposed upon the lawn of an old English country-house, in what I should call the perfect middle of a splendid summer afternoon. Part of the afternoon had waned, but much of it was left, and what was left was of the finest and rarest quality. Real dusk would not arrive for many hours; but the flood of summer light had begun to ebb, the air had grown mellow, the shadows were long upon the smooth, dense turf. They lengthened slowly, however, and the scene expressed that sense of leisure still to come which is perhaps the chief source of one's enjoyment of such a scene at such an hour.

Henry James (1843–1916), from *The Portrait of a Lady*, 1881

Weeding is a delightful occupation, especially after summer rain, when the roots come up clear and clean. One gets to know how many and various are the ways of weeds—as many almost as the moods of human creatures. How easy and pleasant to pull up are the soft annuals like Chickweed and Groundsel, and how one looks with respect at deep-rooted things like Docks, that make one go and fetch a spade.

Gertrude Jekyll (1843–1932), from *Wood and Garden*, 1899

from THE TWO SWANS
(A FAIRY TALE)

And bright and silvery the willows sleep
Over the shady verge—no mad winds tease
Their hoary heads; but quietly they weep
Their sprinkling leaves—half fountains and half trees:
There lilies be—and fairer than all these,
A solitary Swan her breast of snow
Launches against the wave that seems to freeze
Into a chaste reflection, still below
Twin shadow of herself wherever she may go.

Thomas Hood (1799–1845)

Books to read by the water

The Wind in the Willows by Kenneth Grahame

*

Waterlog by Roger Deakin

*

Swallows and Amazons by Arthur Ransome

*

Frenchman's Creek by Daphne du Maurier

*

Three Men in a Boat by Jerome K. Jerome

*

A Sky Painted Gold by Laura Wood

Raspberry-Jam. — Take three parts of picked finest raspberries and one of red currant juice, with equal weight of sugar. Put on half the sugar with a little water; skim this and add the fruit. Boil for fifteen minutes, add the other half of the sugar, and boil for another five minutes, and, when cold, pot the jam. This and all other jams may be made with less sugar, if they are longer boiled: but both colour and quality will suffer in the process. Less boiling will serve if the sugar is previously high-boiled.

Margaret Dods, pseudonym of Christian Isobel Johnstone (1781–1857), from *The Cook and Housewife's Manual*, 1826

'He said the pleasantest manner of spending a hot July day was lying from morning till evening on a bank of heath in the middle of the moors, with the bees humming dreamily about among the bloom, and the larks singing high up overhead, and the blue sky and bright sun shining steadily and cloudlessly. That was his most perfect idea of heaven's happiness: mine was rocking in a rustling green tree, with a west wind blowing, and bright white clouds flitting rapidly above; and not only larks, but throstles, and blackbirds, and linnets, and cuckoos pouring out music on every side, and the moors seen at a distance, broken into cool dusky dells; but close by great swells of long grass undulating in waves to the breeze; and woods and sounding water, and the whole world awake and wild with joy. He wanted all to lie in an ecstasy of peace; I wanted all to sparkle and dance in a glorious jubilee.'

Emily Brontë (1818–1848), from *Wuthering Heights*, 1847

from LOUD WITHOUT THE WIND WAS ROARING

For the moors! For the moors, where the short grass
Like velvet beneath us should lie!
For the moors! For the moors, where each high pass
Rose sunny against the clear sky!

For the moors, where the linnet was trilling
Its song on the old granite stone;
Where the lark, the wild sky-lark, was filling
Every breast with delight like its own!

     Emily Brontë (1818–1848)

Mills and scattered cottages chase romance from these valleys; it is only higher up, deep in amongst the ridges of the moors, that Imagination can find rest for the sole of her foot: and even if she finds it there, she must be a solitude-loving raven — no gentle dove. If she demand beauty to inspire her, she must bring it inborn: these moors are too stern to yield any product so delicate. The eye of the gazer must itself brim with a 'purple light,' intense enough to perpetuate the brief flower-flush of August on the heather, or the rare sunset-smile of June; out of his heart must well the freshness, that in latter spring and early summer brightens the bracken, nurtures the moss, and cherishes the starry flowers that spangle for a few weeks the pasture of the moor-sheep. Unless that light and freshness are innate and self-sustained, the drear prospect of a Yorkshire moor will be found as barren of poetic as of agricultural interest: where the love of wild nature is strong, the locality will perhaps be clung to with the more passionate constancy, because from the hill-lover's self comes half its charm.

My sister Emily loved the moors. Flowers brighter than the rose bloomed in the blackest of the heath for her; out of a sullen hollow in a livid hill-side her mind could make an Eden. She found in the bleak solitude many and dear delights; and not the least and best loved was — liberty.

Liberty was the breath of Emily's nostrils; without it, she perished.

Charlotte Brontë (1816–1855), from the preface to the *Collected Poems*, 1850

In the utter stillness she heard the tinkle of the fountain, and smelled the roses whose blossoms hung rich and motionless. So she drifted, drifted on the wistful feet of beauty, past the water and the swans, to the noble park, where, underneath a great oak, a doe all dappled lay with her four fine feet together, her fawn nestling sun-coloured beside her.

Oh, and this doe was her familiar. It would talk to her, because she was a magician, it would tell her stories as if the sunshine spoke.

> D. H. Lawrence (1885–1930), from *The Rainbow*, 1915

Summer is perfect now.

The wheat says so, when in the dawn it drips with half-an-hour's rain and gleams like copper under the fresh, dim sky; it cries aloud the same when it crackles in the midday sun, and the golden sea of it washes murmurously to the feet of the hills.

In the hedges and fields the agrimony wands and mullein staves, the climbing vetch, the cushioned bird's-foot lotus, the myriads of ragwort and sow thistle, are golden too.

The meadowsweet and honeysuckle flowers and the wild carrot seeds give out sweet scents, but not so strong as not to be drowned, when the wind blows, by a thousand lesser scents from field and wood and farmyard.

Wood pigeons coo in the high-shaded storeys of the beeches and in the wet willow copses where bushes and herbage have grown so dense that hardly a bird's-nester or a lover would care to penetrate them. In the dark wood alleys, all day long, hang insects whose wings seem to be still in their swiftness, like golden lamps.

The gardens have amber lilies, fuchsia trees, phloxes, poppies, hollyhocks, carnations, snap-dragons, rockets and red flax rising above rose of Sharon and lemon-scented balm and yellow stone-crop, where the tortoise-shell butterflies worship with opening wings.

And on the garden walls the purple plums ooze and heave in the sun with yellow wasps that give a touch of horror to the excellent and abounding life of perfect summer.

> Edward Thomas (1878–1917), from *The Heart of England*, 1906

LAVENDER SHORTBREAD

A summer teatime treat, scented with freshly picked lavender from your garden or local lavender farm.

Makes 20 shortbread biscuits

INGREDIENTS

160g (5¾oz) good quality unsalted butter, softened, plus extra for greasing

80g (2¾oz) caster sugar

1 tsp freshly gathered lavender flowers (or ½ tsp dried culinary lavender)

200g (7oz) plain flour

40g (1½oz) cornflour

Plus, a small amount of caster or demerara sugar for sprinkling on shortbread once cooked

METHOD

1. Preheat the oven to 170°C (150°C Fan), 325°F, Gas Mark 3.

2. Grease and base-line a 20 x 20 x 3.5cm (8 x 8 x 1½ inch) non-stick baking tin.

3. Place the softened butter, caster sugar and lavender in a large mixing bowl and beat with a handheld electric mixer until pale and creamy.

4. Sift the plain flour and the cornflour into the butter and sugar mixture.

5. Starting on a low speed so the flour and cornflour don't fly everywhere, beat with the handheld electric mixer until all the ingredients are incorporated and the dough is smooth.

6. Tip the dough onto the greased baking tray and press it out into an even layer with a spatula or palette knife.

7. Prick the dough all over with a fork.

8. Place the tray in a preheated oven and cook for 20 to 25 minutes, or until the top is firm to touch and is a pale biscuit colour.

9. Remove from the oven and, working quickly, sprinkle with caster or demerara sugar and leave to cool for a few minutes.

10. Cut into fingers or squares and carefully remove the shortbread with a palette knife onto a wire rack to finish cooling.

11. Once cold, store the shortbread in an airtight tin.

from **THE GARDEN**

What wond'rous life in this I lead!
Ripe apples drop about my head;
The luscious clusters of the vine
Upon my mouth do crush their wine;
The nectarine and curious peach
Into my hands themselves do reach;
Stumbling on melons as I pass,
Ensnar'd with flow'rs, I fall on grass.

Meanwhile the mind, from pleasure less,
Withdraws into its happiness;
The mind, that ocean where each kind
Does straight its own resemblance find,
Yet it creates, transcending these,
Far other worlds, and other seas;
Annihilating all that's made
To a green thought in a green shade.

ANDREW MARVELL (1621–1678)

Books for the country gardener

Elizabeth and Her German Garden
by Elizabeth von Arnim

*

Old Herbaceous by Reginald Arkell

*

Beatrix Potter's Gardening Life by Marta McDowell

*

The Morville Hours by Katherine Swift

*

My Garden World by Monty Don

*

The Potting Shed Murder
by Paula Sutton

THE SECRET JOY

Face to face with the sunflower,
Cheek to cheek with the rose,
We follow a secret highway
Hardly a traveller knows.
The gold that lies in the folded bloom
Is all our wealth;
We eat of the heart of the forest
With innocent stealth.
We know the ancient roads
In the leaf of a nettle,
And bathe in the blue profound
Of a speedwell petal.

                    MARY WEBB (1881–1927)

There is no month in the whole year in which nature wears a more beautiful appearance than in the month of August. Spring has many beauties, and May is a fresh and blooming month, but the charms of this time of year are enhanced by their contrast with the winter season. August has no such advantage. It comes when we remember nothing but clear skies, green fields, and sweet-smelling flowers — when the recollection of snow, and ice, and bleak winds, has faded from our minds as completely as they have disappeared from the earth — and yet what a pleasant time it is! Orchards and cornfields ring with the hum of labour; trees bend beneath the thick clusters of rich fruit which bow their branches to the ground; and the corn, piled in graceful sheaves, or waving in every light breath that sweeps above it, as if it wooed the sickle, tinges the landscape with a golden hue. A mellow softness appears to hang over the whole earth....

> Charles Dickens (1812–1870), from *The Pickwick Papers*, 1837

For me that will always be the summer day of summer days — a cloudless sky, ditches and roadside deep in grass, poppies, cuckoo pint, trees heavy with leaf, orchards bulging over hedge briars....

Ah those days... for many years afterwards their happiness haunted me. Sometimes, listening to music, I drift back and nothing has changed. The long end of summer. Day after day of warm weather, voices calling as night came on and lighted windows pricked the darkness and, at day-break, the murmur of corn and the warm smell of fields ripe for harvest. And being young.

> J. L. Carr (1912–1994), from *A Month in the Country*, 1980

from AUGUST MOONRISE

The sun was gone, and the moon was coming
Over the blue Connecticut hills;
The west was rosy, the east was flushed,
And over my head the swallows rushed
This way and that, with changeful wills.
I heard them twitter and watched them dart
Now together and now apart
Like dark petals blown from a tree;
The maples stamped against the west
Were black and stately and full of rest,
And the hazy orange moon grew up
And slowly changed to yellow gold
While the hills were darkened, fold on fold
To a deeper blue than a flower could hold.
Down the hill I went, and then
I forgot the ways of men,
For night-scents, heady, and damp and cool
Wakened ecstasy in me
On the brink of a shining pool.

     Sara Teasdale (1884–1933)

SUMMER BEGINS TO HAVE THE LOOK

Summer begins to have the look
Peruser of enchanting Book
Reluctantly but sure perceives
A gain upon the backward leaves —

Autumn begins to be inferred
By millinery of the cloud
Or deeper color in the shawl
That wraps the everlasting hill.

The eye begins its avarice
A meditation chastens speech
Some Dyer of a distant tree
Resumes his gaudy industry.

Conclusion is the course of All
At most to be perennial
And then elude stability
Recalls to immortality.

Emily Dickinson (1830–1886)

3
AUTUMN

RICH DAYS

Welcome to you rich Autumn days,
Ere comes the cold, leaf-picking wind;
When golden stocks are seen in fields,
All standing arm-in-arm entwined;
And gallons of sweet cider seen
On trees in apples red and green.

With mellow pears that cheat our teeth,
Which melt that tongues may suck them in;
With blue-black damsons, yellow plums,
Now sweet and soft from stone to skin;
And woodnuts rich, to make us go
Into the loneliest lanes we know.

W. H. Davies (1871–1940)

from AUTUMN JOURNAL

September has come, it is hers
  Whose vitality leaps in the autumn,
Whose nature prefers
  Trees without leaves and a fire in the fireplace.

LOUIS MACNEICE (1907–1963)

from TO AUTUMN

Season of mists and mellow fruitfulness,
   Close bosom-friend of the maturing sun;
Conspiring with him how to load and bless
   With fruit the vines that round the thatch-eves run;
To bend with apples the moss'd cottage-trees,
   And fill all fruit with ripeness to the core;
     To swell the gourd, and plump the hazel shells
   With a sweet kernel; to set budding more,
And still more, later flowers for the bees,
Until they think warm days will never cease,
   For summer has o'er-brimm'd their clammy cells.

                         John Keats (1795–1821)

The windows were thrown wide open, and the fresh country air blew in upon them as they dined. The weather was lovely; the foliage of the woods touched here and there with faint gleams of the earliest tints of autumn; the yellow corn still standing in some of the fields, in others just falling under the shining sickle; while in the narrow lanes you met great wagons drawn by broad-chested cart-horses, carrying home the rich golden store. To any one who has been, during the hot summer months, pent up in London, there is in the first taste of rustic life a kind of sensuous rapture scarcely to be described.

Mary Elizabeth Braddon (1835–1915), from *Lady Audley's Secret*, 1862

A lovely autumnal day; the air soft, balmy, genial; the sky of that softened and delicate blue upon which the eye loves to rest,—the blue which gives such relief to the rich beauty of the earth, all around glowing in the ripe and mellow tints of the most gorgeous of the seasons. Really such an autumn may well compensate our English climate for the fine spring of the south, that spring of which the poets talk, but which we so seldom enjoy. Such an autumn glows upon us like a splendid evening; it is the very sunset of the year…

Mary Russell Mitford (1787–1855), from *Our Village*, 1824

It was a September evening and all the gaps and clearings in the woods were brimmed up with ruby sunset light.

L. M. Montgomery (1874–1942), from *Anne of Green Gables*, 1908

In Meryton they parted; the two youngest repaired to the lodgings of one of the officers' wives, and Elizabeth continued her walk alone, crossing field after field at a quick pace, jumping over stiles and springing over puddles with impatient activity, and finding herself at last within view of the house, with weary ankles, dirty stockings, and a face glowing with the warmth of exercise.

Jane Austen (1775–1817), from *Pride and Prejudice*, 1813

My green-house is never so pleasant as when we are just upon the point of being turned out of it. The gentleness of the autumnal suns, and the calmness of this latter season, make it a much more agreeable retreat than we ever find it in the summer; when, the winds being generally brisk, we cannot cool it by admitting a sufficient quantity of air, without being at the same time incommoded by it. But now I sit with all the windows and the door wide open, and am regaled with the scent of every flower, in a garden as full of flowers as I have known how to make it. We keep no bees, but if I lived in a hive, I should hardly hear more of their music. All the bees in the neighbourhood resort to a bed of mignonette, opposite to the window, and pay me for the honey they get out of it by a hum, which, though rather monotonous, is as agreeable to my ear as the whistling of my linnets.

William Cowper (1731–1800), 18 September 1784

The autumn trees gleam in the yellow moonlight, in the light of harvest moons, the light which mellows the energy of labour, and smooths the stubble, and brings the wave lapping blue to the shore.

Virginia Woolf (1882–1941), from *To the Lighthouse*, 1927

from THE GARDEN IN SEPTEMBER

Now thin mists temper the slow-ripening beams
Of the September sun: his golden gleams
On gaudy flowers shine, that prank the rows
Of high-grown hollyhocks, and all tall shows
That Autumn flaunteth in his bushy bowers;
Where tomtits, hanging from the drooping heads
Of giant sunflowers, peck the nutty seeds;
And in the feathery aster bees on wing
Seize and set free the honied flowers,
Till thousand stars leap with their visiting:
While ever across the path mazily flit,
Unpiloted in the sun,
The dreamy butterflies
With dazzling colours powdered and soft glooms,
White, black and crimson stripes, and peacock eyes,
Or on chance flowers sit,
With idle effort plundering one by one
The nectaries of deepest-throated blooms.

      Robert Bridges (1844–1930)

She could not stay in the garden. The hollyhocks and the asters and the late roses all seemed to be waiting for something to happen. It was one of those still, shiny autumn days, when everything does seem to be waiting.

> Edith Nesbit (1858–1924), from *The Railway Children*, 1905

Hop-picking goes on without the least interruption. Stone-curlews cry late in the evenings. The congregating flocks of *hirundines* on the church & tower are very beautiful, & amusing! When they fly-off altogether from the Roof, on any alarm, they quite swarm in the air. But they soon settle in heaps, & preening their feathers, & lifting up their wings to admit the sun, seem highly to enjoy the warm situation. Thus they spend the heat of the day, preparing for their emigration, &, as it were consulting when & where they are to go. The flight about the church seems to consist chiefly of house-martins, about 400 in number: but there are other places of rendezvous about the village frequented at the same time. The swallows seem to delight more in holding their assemblies on trees.

> Gilbert White (1720–1793), 14 September 1791

As a house, Barton Cottage, though small, was comfortable and compact; but as a cottage it was defective, for the building was regular, the roof was tiled, the window shutters were not painted green, nor were the walls covered with honeysuckles. A narrow passage led directly through the house into the garden behind. On each side of the entrance was a sitting room, about sixteen feet square; and beyond them were the offices and the stairs.

Four bed-rooms and two garrets formed the rest of the house. It had not been built many years and was in good repair. In comparison of Norland, it was poor and small indeed!—but the tears which recollection called forth as they entered the house were soon dried away. They were cheered by the joy of the servants on their arrival, and each for the sake of the others resolved to appear happy. It was very early in September; the season was fine, and from first seeing the place under the advantage of good weather, they received an impression in its favour which was of material service in recommending it to their lasting approbation.

    Jane Austen (1775–1817), from *Sense and Sensibility*, 1811

Outside in the sunshine everything shimmers. Gold falls in splashes on the branches of the elm, and the beechwoods are turning a burnt brown. Scarlet berries spot the hedgerows, converting the red of the Devon earth to a dull crimson. Away on the open stretches of Dartmoor, the wind is already bleak and unfriendly and the ponies huddle for warmth at night under the stunted bushes; but here in this soft land of shelter, where, round and sudden as a child's imaginings, rise the little wooded hills, the autumn is still kind in its touch. It is gentle and golden, and if a few leaves have started to fall from the trees, it must have been by accident. There is as yet no hint of winter, for the film of frost upon the ricks vanishes when the sun rises. When it beats upon the hedgerows the dewdrops disappear from the spiders' webs that bind one curl of traveller's joy to the next.

    Clare Leighton (1898–1989), from *The Farmer's Year*, 1933

Hay Fair. Roads lively with men, horses and sheep. We were busy all day dressing the Church or preparing decorations. Mrs. Price and Miss Elcox had got a quantity of wild hops from their fields and were arranging bright red apples for ornament. Also they had boughs loaded with rosy apples and quantities of bright yellow Siberian crabs… Gibbins undertook the font and dressed it very tastefully with moss and white asters under the sweeping fronds of the silver fern. Round the stem were twined the delicate light green sprays of white convolvulus. The pillars were wreathed and twined with wild hop vine falling in graceful careless festoons and curling tendrils from wreath and capital. St. Andrew crossed sheaves of all sorts of corn were placed against the walls between the windows, wheat, barley and oats with a spray of hop vine drooping in a festoon across the sheaf butts and a spray of red barberries between the sheaf heads. Bright flowers in pots clustered round the spring of the arches upon the capitals of the pillars, the flower pots veiled by a twist of hop vine.

The Reverend Francis Kilvert (1840–1879), 15 September 1870

For a harvest supper, tables are set down the length of the barn and all the hands on the farm, together with their wives, are invited. The repast, in which beef and mutton, bread and cheese and beer, figure on an ample scale, is of course the main feature of the entertainment; when this important and lengthy business has been discussed, the lighter items on the programme follow. Pipes are lighted, glasses replenished, speeches and songs are delivered. I say 'delivered' advisedly in connection with the latter, which are, for the most part, ancient ditties, scarce fit for repetition here, treating of the follies and sorrows of too-confiding village maidens.

Eleanor G. Hayden (1865–1954), from *Travels Round Our Village*, 1901

from SEPTEMBER

There are twelve months throughout the year,
From January to December—
And the primest month of all the twelve
Is the merry month of September!
Then apples so red
Hang overhead,
And nuts ripe-brown
Come showering down
In the bountiful days of September!

There are flowers enough in the summer-time,
More flowers than I can remember—
But none with the purple, gold, and red
That dye the flowers of September!
The gorgeous flowers of September!
And the sun looks through
A clearer blue,
And the moon at night
Sheds a clearer light
On the beautiful flowers of September!

MARY HOWITT (1799—1888)

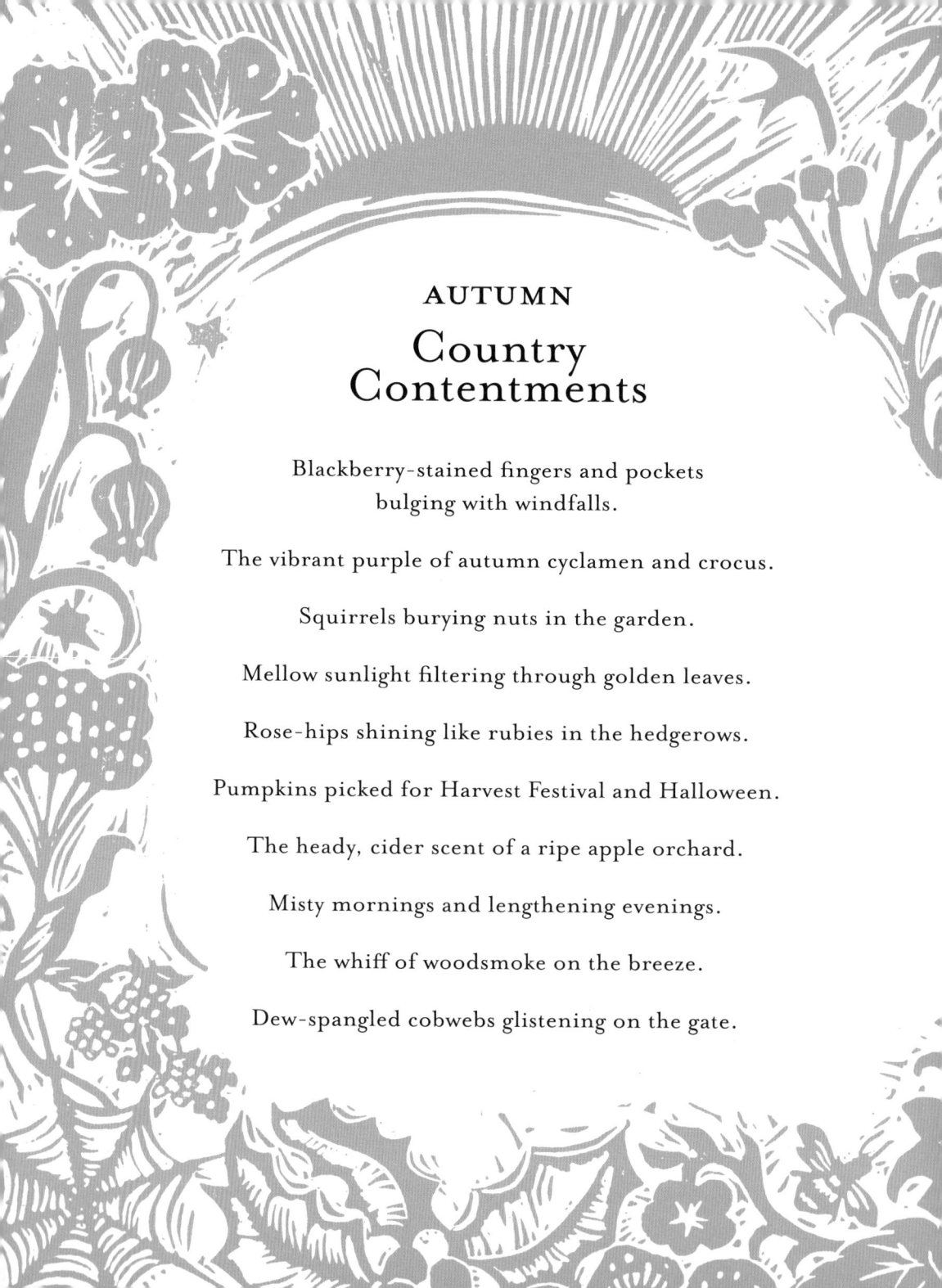

AUTUMN
Country Contentments

Blackberry-stained fingers and pockets bulging with windfalls.

The vibrant purple of autumn cyclamen and crocus.

Squirrels burying nuts in the garden.

Mellow sunlight filtering through golden leaves.

Rose-hips shining like rubies in the hedgerows.

Pumpkins picked for Harvest Festival and Halloween.

The heady, cider scent of a ripe apple orchard.

Misty mornings and lengthening evenings.

The whiff of woodsmoke on the breeze.

Dew-spangled cobwebs glistening on the gate.

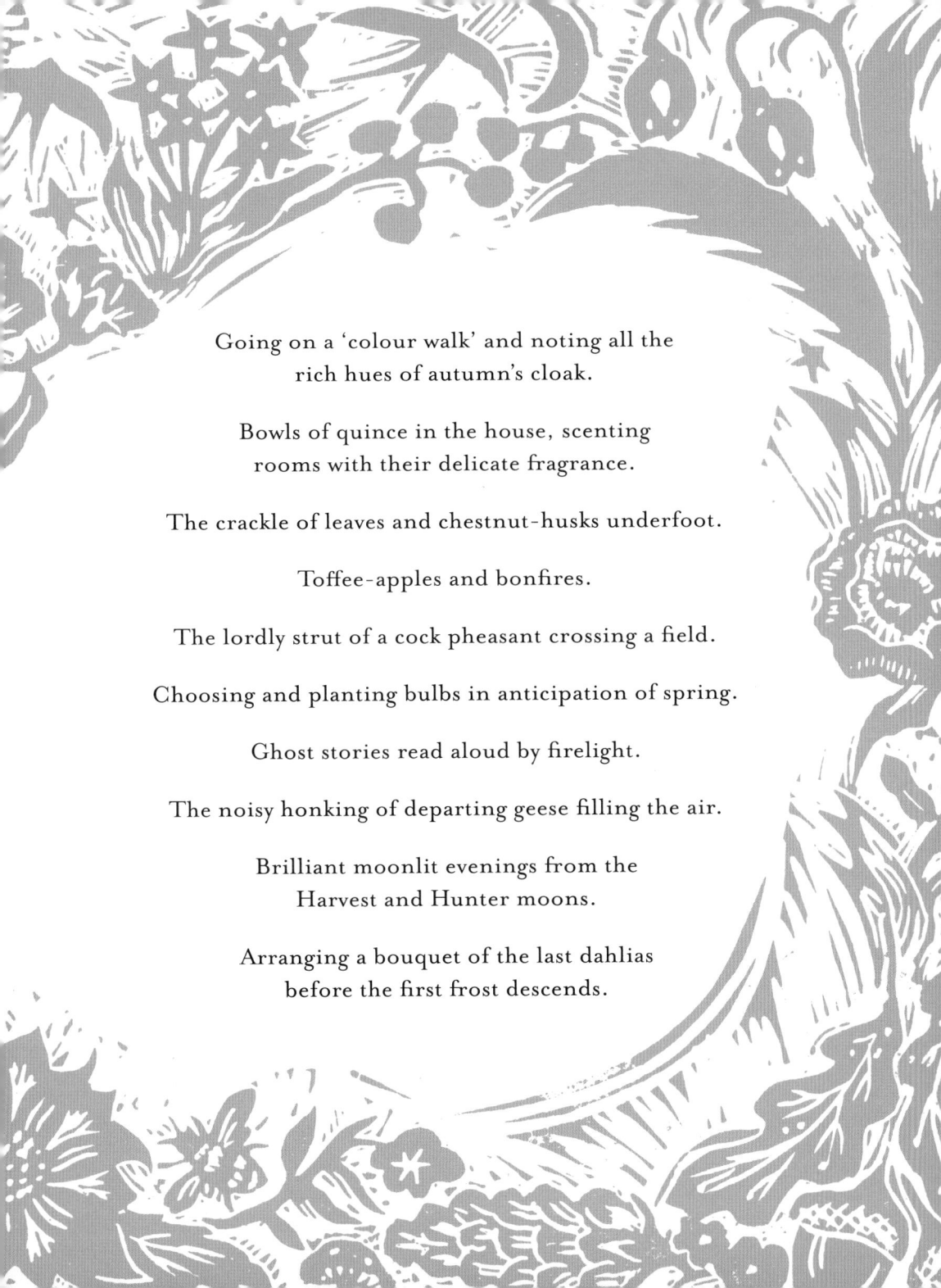

Going on a 'colour walk' and noting all the rich hues of autumn's cloak.

Bowls of quince in the house, scenting rooms with their delicate fragrance.

The crackle of leaves and chestnut-husks underfoot.

Toffee-apples and bonfires.

The lordly strut of a cock pheasant crossing a field.

Choosing and planting bulbs in anticipation of spring.

Ghost stories read aloud by firelight.

The noisy honking of departing geese filling the air.

Brilliant moonlit evenings from the Harvest and Hunter moons.

Arranging a bouquet of the last dahlias before the first frost descends.

AUTUMN GILT

The late September sunshine,
Lime green on the linden leaves,
Burns bronze on the slated roof-tops,
Yellow on the farmer's last sheaves.

It flares flame-like on the fire hydrant,
Is ebony on the blackbird's wing,
Blue beryl on the face of the ocean,
Glints gold on the bride's wedding ring.

A sparkling rainbow on the stained-glass window,
It's a silver sheen on the kitchen sink,
The late September sunshine,
Is a chameleon, I think.

                        Valerie Bloom (1956–)

from THE EARTHLY PARADISE

About the edges of the yellow corn,
And o'er the gardens grown somewhat outworn
The bees went hurrying to fill up their store;
The apple-boughs bent over more and more;
With peach and apricot the garden wall,
Was odorous, and the pears began to fall
From off the high tree with each freshening breeze.

William Morris (1834–1896)

The light air seemed full of powdered gold; below the dewy bloom of the lawns the woodlands blushed and smouldered, and the hills across the river swam in molten blue.

>   Edith Wharton (1862–1937), from *The House of Mirth*, 1905

In every Autumn the farmhouse, with its old tiles and new and its glowing bricks… seems, in spite of its age, to be a great new flower. It is the royal flower of autumn. It expresses at once all that fruit and flower upon the hill have been expressing laboriously and word by word.

Perfect gay youth and sage antiquity are mingled in the aspect of the house… In winter it is old; it has apparently been long fortifying itself against the foreign cold of the landscape, snowy white or windy grey. In spring it is old; the green garlands it as in tender mockery. In summer it is old; it is impatient of the bragging rose on its walls and the multiplication of leaf and flower. But in September it is at home, as if after an exile; it remembers only pleasant things—the autumns of two centuries, their harvest, their fruit, their blossom, their hedgerow vintages of bryony and cornel and thorn, their ruddy moons. Gathered about it are the farm buildings of the same colour, stacks of dark hay, sharp-breasted ricks of corn, maternal, warm oast-houses and orchard and garden, all of the same family.

>   Edward Thomas (1878–1917), from *The Heart of England*, 1906

She still had one great day every year, when, every autumn, the dealer came to purchase the produce of her beehives. Then, in her pantry doorway, a large muslin bag was suspended to drain the honey from the broken pieces of comb into a large, red pan which stood beneath, while, on her doorstep, the end house children waited to see 'the honeyman' carry out and weigh the whole combs. One year —one never-to-be-forgotten year—he had handed to each of them a rich, dripping fragment of comb. He never did it again; but they always waited, for the hope was almost as sweet as the honey.

Flora Thompson (1876–1947), from *Lark Rise*, 1939

Last night I jogged around the Herefordshire lanes and came home almost drunk with the scent of apples. Every breath was a slug of strong cider, at once sweet and dry, fizzy and still: all the contradictions of smell bundled into easy associations of taste. Not enough mention is made of the way that smell is such a feature of the countryside, such as the foetid sweetness of May blossom, the chaffy greenness of haymaking, the strawness of harvest time and hard boniness of frost on the nose. I know that this might seem like a catalogue of rural elitism, but city gardens serve as *rus in urbe* now more than ever, and for most people the closest contact with the earthiness of country matters is through our gardens. That tang of apple from the little tree in your garden at this time of year is the same experience as mine last night.

Monty Don (1955–), from *The Ivington Diaries*, 2010

SOMETHING TOLD THE WILD GEESE

Something told the wild geese
It was time to go.
Though the fields lay golden
Something whispered, — 'Snow.'
Leaves were green and stirring,
Berries, luster-glossed,
But beneath warm feathers
Something cautioned, — 'Frost.'
All the sagging orchards
Steamed with amber spice,
But each wild breast stiffened
At remembered ice.
Something told the wild geese
It was time to fly, —
Summer sun was on their wings,
Winter in their cry.

Rachel Field (1894–1942)

Books to read under an apple tree

Twelve Words for Moss by Elizabeth-Jane Burnett

*

Orchard: A Year in England's Eden
by Benedict Macdonald and Nicholas Gates

*

The Wood by John Lewis-Stempel

*

A Home for All Seasons by Gavin Plumley

*

The Apple: A Delicious History by Sally Coulthard

*

The Woodlanders by Thomas Hardy

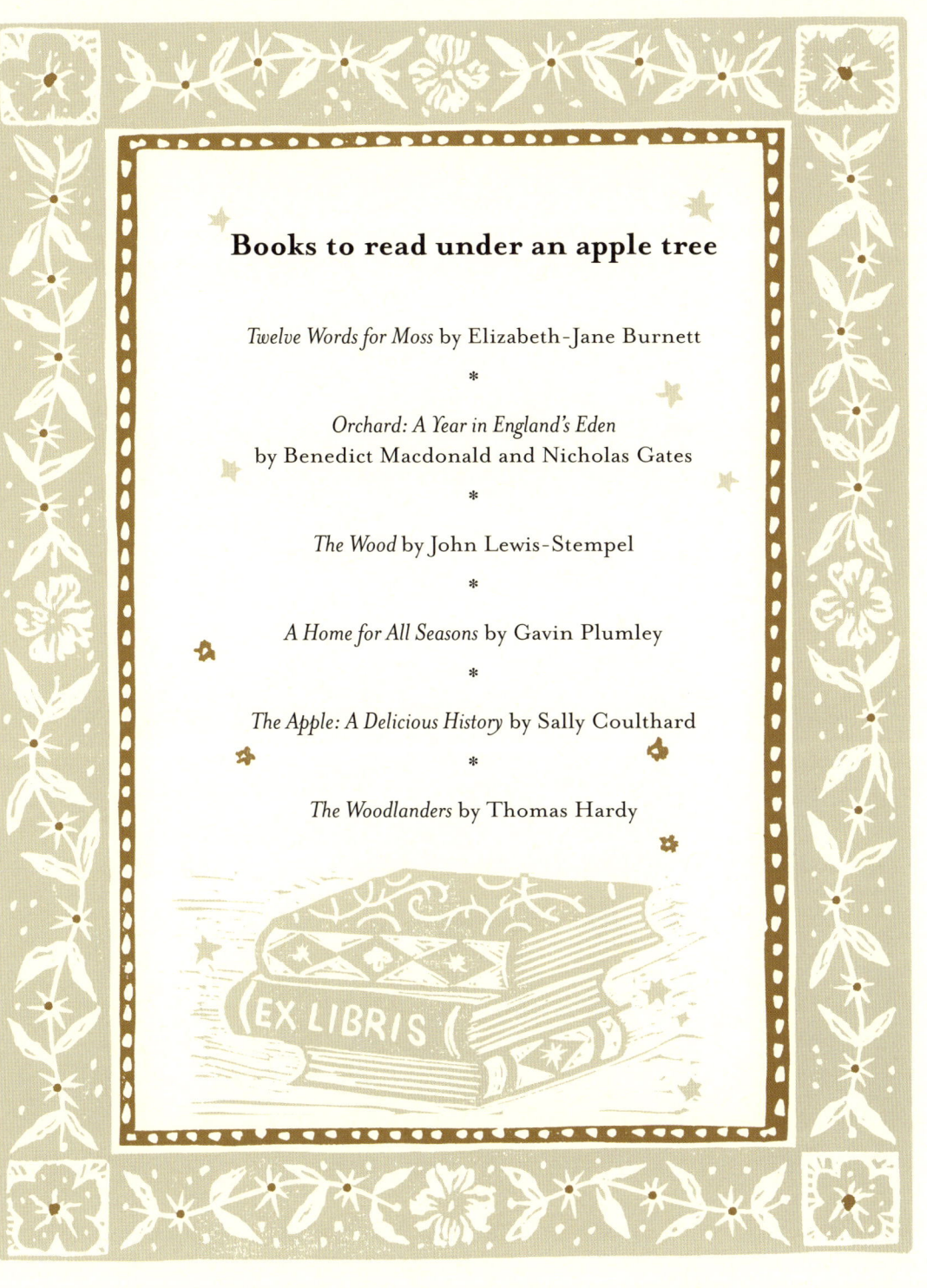

MOONLIT APPLES

At the top of the house the apples are laid in rows,
And the skylight lets the moonlight in, and those
Apples are deep-sea apples of green. There goes
A cloud on the moon in the autumn night.

A mouse in the wainscot scratches, and scratches, and then
There is no sound at the top of the house of men
Or mice; and the cloud is blown, and the moon again
Dapples the apples with deep-sea light.

They are lying in rows there, under the gloomy beams;
On the sagging floor; they gather the silver streams
Out of the moon, those moonlit apples of dreams,
And quiet is the steep stair under.

In the corridors under there is nothing but sleep.
And stiller than ever on orchard boughs they keep
Tryst with the moon, and deep is the silence, deep
On moon-washed apples of wonder.

JOHN DRINKWATER (1882—1937)

There were a great many holidays at Plumfield, and one of the most delightful was the yearly apple-picking. For then the Marches, Laurences, Brookes and Bhaers turned out in full force and made a day of it. Five years after Jo's wedding, one of these fruitful festivals occurred, a mellow October day, when the air was full of an exhilarating freshness which made the spirits rise and the blood dance healthily in the veins. The old orchard wore its holiday attire. Goldenrod and asters fringed the mossy walls. Grasshoppers skipped briskly in the sere grass, and crickets chirped like fairy pipers at a feast. Squirrels were busy with their small harvesting. Birds twittered their adieux from the alders in the lane, and every tree stood ready to send down its shower of red or yellow apples at the first shake. Everybody was there. Everybody laughed and sang, climbed up and tumbled down. Everybody declared that there never had been such a perfect day or such a jolly set to enjoy it, and everyone gave themselves up to the simple pleasures of the hour as freely as if there were no such things as care or sorrow in the world.

    Louisa May Alcott (1832–1888), from *Good Wives*, 1869

In October I went a-graping to the river meadows, and loaded myself with clusters more precious for their beauty and fragrance than for food. There too I admired, though I did not gather, the cranberries, small waxen gems, pendants of the meadow grass, pearly and red… The barberry's brilliant fruit was likewise food for my eyes merely; but I collected a small store of wild apples for coddling…

    Henry David Thoreau (1817–1862), from *Walden*, 1854

from OCTOBER
(THE SHEPHERD'S CALENDAR)

Wild shines each hedge in autumn's gay parade;
And, where the eldern trees to autumn fade,
The glossy berry picturesquely cleaves
Its swarthy bunches 'mid the yellow leaves,
On which the tootling robin feeds at will,
And coy hedge-sparrow stains its little bill.

John Clare (1793–1864)

from **WILD PEACHES**

The autumn frosts will lie upon the grass
Like bloom on grapes of purple-brown and gold.
The misted early mornings will be cold;
The little puddles will be roofed with glass.
The sun, which burns from copper into brass,
Melts these at noon, and makes the boys unfold
Their knitted mufflers; full as they can hold
Fat pockets dribble chestnuts as they pass.

Elinor Wylie (1885–1928)

Roast apples also were October's fare, and every night there was a dish of apples, roasted to the exact pitch when the skin burst and the white foam of apple spilt out. 'A kiss' it was called. They were carried from the oven to the tea-table, and served with a large jug of thick cream, and a bowl of castor sugar. So I follow this tradition, for I grow the particular kind of apples with thin skin and pointed shape which make this delicate froth, and I have them for high tea. They were not served for any other meal, they were too delicate and too uncertain of their time of bursting.

                Alison Uttley (1884–1976), from *A Year in the Country*, 1957

October is the month when the brew-houses and the cider-presses are as hard at work in the north as are the wine vats in southern countries. At the time of year when the burst berries of the spindle tree are showing orange and pink in the hedges it would not be possible to walk five miles through the lanes of Somerset without becoming aware that it is the cider-making season. In dim, wasp-drunken orchards, the poetical fruit… lies piled up in massed heaps under great trees so old that they might very well have been saplings during the spring months of the Duke of Monmouth's adventure, so leaned down do their grey trunks look and so drooping with the years their crooked boughs. I have seen cider-presses in remote farms that must have been squeezing out the delicious juices of famous Somersetshire apples such as Trasks, Taunton Blacks, and Jack Horners, season after season since the eighteenth century. The crushing process is assisted by laying the apples on straw, and, after the last drop of brown syrup has been strained off, the residue of pulp, a cider-cake, is tossed on the ground for the cattle to nuzzle at.

                Llewelyn Powys (1884–1939), from *The Twelve Months*, 1936

A IS FOR APPLE... A LIST OF APPLE VARIETIES WITH UNUSUAL NAMES

Adams's Pearmain
Annie Elizabeth
Beauty of Kent
Bedfordshire Foundling
Bess Pool
Betty Geeson
Blenheim Orange
Bramley's Seedling
Calville Blanc d'Hiver
Catshead
Court of Wick
Cox's Orange Pippin
D'Arcy Spice
Devonshire Quarrenden
Duchess's Favourite
Duck's Bill
Early Julyan
Fearn's Pippin
Golden Pippin
Grenadier

Hawthornden
Irish Peach
Kentish Fillbasket
Lamb Abbey Pearmain
Lord Derby
Peasgood's Nonsuch
Pomeroy
Pott's Seedling
Roxbury Russet
Scarlet Nonpareil
Schoolmaster
Scotch Bridget
Sops-in-Wine
Stirling Castle
Summer Golden Pippin
Tom Putt
Tower of Glamis
Warner's King
Wheeler's Russet
Yorkshire Greening

BAKED APPLES

A simple dessert that makes itself. If you can, use cooking apples from your own apple tree or a local apple stand.

Makes 4 baked apples

INGREDIENTS

4 cooking apples (Bramleys are an excellent choice)

60g (2oz) light muscovado sugar

30g (1oz) sultanas

30g (1oz) raisins

1 tsp cinnamon

½ tsp mixed spice

50g (1¾oz) unsalted butter, divided into 8 slices

150ml (5¼fl oz) apple juice

To serve

Single cream or vanilla ice cream

METHOD

1. Preheat the oven to 180°C (160°C Fan), 350°F, Gas Mark 4.
2. Wash and dry the apples, then using an apple corer or sharp knife, core them very nearly to the bottom, but leave the base intact, making sure to remove any seeds.
3. Using a sharp knife, draw a circle around the circumference of each apple so they do not burst as they cook.
4. Stand the apples in a baking dish.
5. In a bowl, mix together the sugar, dried fruits and spices.
6. Press one of the slices of butter in the bottom of each apple.
7. Lightly pack each apple with a quarter of the sugar, dried fruit and spice mixture. Then top each apple with another slice of butter.
8. Pour the apple juice around the apples, and place the dish in the preheated oven. Baste the apples with the apple juice after 15 minutes in the oven.
9. Cook for another 15–20 minutes more (30–35 minutes in total) or until the apples are soft right through when pierced with a skewer, but still holding their shape.
10. Remove from the oven and let the apples cool slightly before serving. Serve with a generous drizzle of single cream or a scoop of vanilla ice cream.

Books for the country cook

The Great Dixter Cookbook: Recipes from an English Garden by Aaron Bertelsen

✼

Home Made: Recipes from the Countryside by Kate Humble

✼

The Farm Table by Julius Roberts

✼

Good Food on the Aga by Ambrose Heath

✼

The Country Housewife's Book by Lucy H. Yates

✼

Recipes from an Old Farmhouse by Alison Uttley

Apple-Pie: Wipe, pare, and slice the apples; core with the instrument. Lay a strip of puff-paste round the edge of the dish. Put in a layer of the sliced fruit, then sugar and whatever seasonings you use. A small mixture of quince greatly improves the flavour. Proceed in this manner till the dish is heaped, keeping the fruit highest in the middle. Cover it with puff-paste, ornament the border and the top with leaves, flowers, etc. — Obs. A variety of apples besides codlins are used for baking, though russetings, Ribstone pippins, golden pippins, and such as melt equally, and are a little acid, are esteemed the best. Apple-pie used to be seasoned with pounded cinnamon and cloves; now lemon-grate, quince, marmalade, candied citron, or orange peel, are preferred. If the apples have become dry and insipid, the parings and cores may be boiled with a stick of cinnamon and sugar, and the strained liquor added to the pie. Apple-pie is often liked hot. It is eaten with plain cream, made cream, or Creme Patissiere… It was wont to be buttered; and this is still the practice in some provincial situations in England, though buttered pease, and buttered apple-pie, for reasons which we do not comprehend, have latterly come to be considered ungenteel, if not absolutely vulgar. Buttering is performed by putting a piece of fresh butter into the hot pie when it is cut open. Apples must be thrown into plenty of water as they are pared, or they will become discoloured.

>   Margaret Dods, pseudonym of Christian Isobel Johnstone (1781–1857), from *The Cook and Housewife's Manual*, 1826

We have just had two hampers of apples from Kintbury, and the floor of our little garret is almost covered.

>   Jane Austen (1775–1817), from a letter to Cassandra Austen, 24 October 1808

Is not this a true autumn day? Just the still melancholy that I love – that makes life and nature harmonise. The birds are consulting about their migrations, the trees are putting on the hectic or the pallid hues of decay, and begin to strew the ground, that one's very footsteps may not disturb the repose of earth and air, while they give us a scent that is a perfect anodyne to the restless spirit. Delicious autumn! My very soul is wedded to it, and if I were a bird I would fly about the earth seeking the successive autumns.

George Eliot (1819–1880), from a letter to Miss Lewis, 1 October 1841

Saturday, 7th October. – Charming weather. The woods on the hills are glorious in the sunshine, the golden light playing about their leafy crests, as though it took pleasure in kindling such rich coloring. The red of the oaks grows deeper, the chestnuts are of a brighter gold color. Still a touch of green in the woods; the foliage of the beech struggles a long time to preserve its verdure, the brownish yellow creeps over it very slowly; most trees turn more rapidly, as though they took pleasure in the change…

Beautiful moonlight this evening, with a decided frosty feeling in the air. The moon was determined to show us what she could do toward lighting up the autumn foliage at night; the effect was singular, as seen in the trees about the lawn. A dreamy fugitive coloring of scarlet and yellow seemed to be thrown over the sumachs and maples, near the house; and even upon the hills, in spots where the light fell with all its power, the difference between the colored belts of yellow or scarlet, and the darker evergreens, was quite perceptible.

Susan Fenimore Cooper (1813–1894), from *Rural Hours*, 1850

FALL, LEAVES, FALL

Fall, leaves, fall; die, flowers, away;
Lengthen night and shorten day;
Every leaf speaks bliss to me
Fluttering from the autumn tree.
I shall smile when wreaths of snow
Blossom where the rose should grow;
I shall sing when night's decay
Ushers in a drearier day.

Emily Brontë (1818–1848)

NORTH WIND IN OCTOBER

In the golden glade the chestnuts are fallen all;
From the sered boughs of the oak the acorns fall:
The beech scatters her ruddy fire;
The lime hath stripped to the cold,
And standeth naked above her yellow attire:
The larch thinneth her spire
To lay the ways of the wood with cloth of gold.

Out of the golden-green and white
Of the brake the fir-trees stand upright
In the forest of flame, and wave aloft
To the blue of heaven their blue-green tuftings soft.

But swiftly in shuddering gloom the splendours fail,
As the harrying North-wind beareth
A cloud of skirmishing hail
The grievèd woodland to smite:
In a hurricane through the trees he teareth,
Raking the boughs and the leaves rending,
And whistleth to the descending
Blows of his icy flail.
Gold and snow he mixeth in spite,
And whirleth afar; as away on his winnowing flight
He passeth, and all again for awhile is bright.

Robert Bridges (1844–1930)

It was one of those still and lovely autumn days when the red and yellow leaves are hanging-pegs to dewy, brilliant gossamer-webs; when the hedges are full of trailing brambles, loaded with ripe blackberries; when the air is full of the farewell whistles and pipes of birds, clear and short—not the long full-throated warbles of spring; when the whirr of the partridge's wings is heard in the stubble-fields, as the sharp hoof-blows fall on the paved lanes; when here and there a leaf floats and flutters down to the ground, although there is not a single breath of wind.

Elizabeth Gaskell (1810–1865), from *Wives and Daughters*, 1866

The lawn is the leaves' dancing floor. I like to stand leaning over the wall above, watching them. The wind is their music and impulse; it is billowing the trees with half a gale. There are leaves from the creeper on the house, scarlet, like soldiers, and green leaves, fresh as summer, from the lime. Away they go, and even the dowager leaves of sober brown and silver grey awake and scamper after them in a gallopade. Then the gust dies, and they stand in groups stirring as in conversation. The wind swoops again; some run to the middle and the rest form a wide circle and revolve round them.

Adrian Bell (1901–1980), from *A Countryman's Autumn Notebook*, 2024

The summer had turned, the summer had gone; the autumn had dropped upon Bly and had blown out half our lights. The place, with its grey sky and withered garlands, its bared spaces and scattered dead leaves, was like a theatre after the performance — all strewn with crumpled playbills.

Henry James (1843–1916), from *The Turn of the Screw*, 1898

As the sun rose I watched a proud ash tree shedding its leaves after a night of frost. It let them go by threes and tens and twenties; very rarely, with little intervals, only one at a time; once or twice a hundred in one flight. Leaflet—for they fall by leaflets—and stalk twirled through the windless air as if they would have liked to fall not quite so rapidly as their companions to that brown and shining and oblivious carpet below. A gentle wind arose from the north and the leaves all went sloping in larger companies to the ground—falling, falling, whispering as they joined the fallen, they fell for a longer time than a poppy spends in opening and shedding its husk in June. But soon only two leaves were left vibrating. In a little while they also, both together, make the leap, twinkling for a short space and then shadowed and lastly bright and silent on the grass. Then the tree stood up entirely bereaved and without a voice, in the silver light of the morning that was still young, and wrote once more its grief in complicated scribble upon a sky of intolerably lustrous pearl.

Edward Thomas (1878–1917), from *The Heart of England*, 1906

In the morning when I arose the mists were hanging over the opposite hills, and the tops of the highest hills were covered with snow. There was a most lively combination at the head of the vale of the yellow autumnal hills wrapped in sunshine, and overhung with partial mists, the green and yellow trees, and the distant snow-topped mountains. It was a most heavenly morning.

Dorothy Wordsworth (1771–1855), Friday 10 October 1800

LEAVES

Myriads and myriads plumed their glittering wings,
As fine as any bird that soars and sings,
As bright as fireflies or the dragon-flies
Or birds of paradise.

Myriads and myriads waved their sheeny fans,
Soft as the dove's breast, or the pelican's;
And some were gold, and some were green, and some
Pink-lipped, like apple-bloom.

A low wind tossed the plumage all one way,
Rippled the gold feathers, and green and gray —
A low wind that in moving sang one song
All day and all night long.

Some trees hung lanterns out, and some had stars
Silver as Hesper, and rose-red as Mars;
A low wind flung the lanterns low and high —
A low wind like a sigh.

KATHARINE TYNAN (1859—1931)

ON THE FIRST LEAVES OF AUTUMN

Between hot chocolate and pumpkin spice,
mellow warmth and misty mornings,

the gold of your mother shines
alongside your father's glowing smile.

Your grandmother bakes buttery cookies,
while your grandfather rakes the amber-
    orange garden.
In a season where everything leaves,
you learn the fine art of loving and letting go.

                           Nikita Gill (1987–)

INDULGENT HOT CHOCOLATE FOR TWO

A delicious hot drink to enjoy by the fire on a chilly autumn day.

To make two hot chocolates

INGREDIENTS

500ml (17fl oz) whole milk

1 tbsp caster sugar (less or more to taste)

¼ tsp vanilla extract

¼ tsp ground cardamom

2 tbsp cocoa powder, sieved

25g (1oz) milk chocolate, finely chopped

25g (1oz) semisweet chocolate, finely chopped

For the topping

Whipped cream and/or grated chocolate (optional)

METHOD

1 Heat the milk, sugar, vanilla extract, ground cardamom, sieved cocoa powder and chocolate pieces gently over a medium heat in a small, non-stick milk pan, using a non-stick silicone-coated whisk to ensure any lumps are dissolved.

2 Once the chocolate has melted and the mixture is smooth and steaming, remove from the heat and divide between two mugs.

3 Top with whipped cream and some grated chocolate for an extra touch of indulgence if desired!

DUSK IN AUTUMN

The moon is like a scimitar,
A little silver scimitar,
A-drifting down the sky.
And near beside it is a star,
A timid twinkling golden star,
That watches like an eye.

And thro' the nursery window-pane
The witches have a fire again,
Just like the ones we make,—
And now I know they're having tea,
I wish they'd give a cup to me,
With witches' currant cake.

SARA TEASDALE (1884—1933)

GINGER SPICE

Sphagnum fuscum, Rusty Bog-moss

Crackle of shoots, pheasant's roost,
sun flushing over hummocks
a ginger, a peach, a flummox of oranges
peeling, that flourishing feeling, to be
brought to life again by the spice
in a stem, to be called to earth again
by a flash in the fen, autumn colours
fusing, burnished bracken moving on
a blackened spine, polishing the rind.

Elizabeth-Jane Burnett (1980–)

October was a beautiful month at Green Gables, when the birches in the hollow turned as golden as sunshine and the maples behind the orchard were royal crimson and the wild cherry trees along the lane put on the loveliest shades of dark red and bronzy green, while the fields sunned themselves in aftermaths.

Anne reveled in the world of color about her.

'Oh, Marilla,' she exclaimed one Saturday morning, coming dancing in with her arms full of gorgeous boughs, 'I'm so glad I live in a world where there are Octobers. It would be terrible if we just skipped from September to November, wouldn't it? Look at these maple branches. Don't they give you a thrill — several thrills? I'm going to decorate my room with them.'

L. M. Montgomery (1874–1942), from *Anne of Green Gables*, 1908

Frost, and sunshine after had reddened the hawthorn sprays, and already they could see through the upper branches—red with haws—for the grass was strewn with the leaves from the exposed tops of the bushes. On the orange maples there were bunches of rosy-winged keys. There was a gloss on the holly leaf, and catkins at the tips of the leafless birch. As the leaves fell from the horse-chestnut boughs the varnished sheaths of the buds for next year appeared; so there were green buds on the willows, black tips to the ash saplings, green buds on the sycamores....

Thin threads of gossamer gleamed, the light ran along their loops as they were lifted by the breeze, and the sky was blue over the buff oaks. Jays screeched in the oaks looking for acorns, and there came the muffled tinkle of a sheep-bell.

Richard Jefferies (1848–1887), from *Bevis*, 1882

LATE OCTOBER

Carefully
the leaves of autumn
sprinkle down the tinny
sound of little dyings
and skies sated
of ruddy sunsets
of roseate dawns
roil ceaselessly in
cobweb greys and turn
to black
for comfort.

Only lovers
see the fall
a signal end to endings
a gruffish gesture alerting
those who will not be alarmed
that we begin to stop
in order to begin
again.

      Maya Angelou (1928–2014)

AUTUMN TRADITIONAL COUNTRY WISDOM

He that would eat fruit must climb the tree.

If there's ice in November that'll bear a duck,
There'll be nothing after but sludge and muck.

Onion's skin very thin,
Mild winter coming in;
Onion's skin thick and tough,
Coming winter cold and rough.

Rowan tree or reed
Put witches to their speed.

If you wish to live and thrive,
Let a spider run alive.

In Autumn if the leaves still hold,
The Winter will be wet and cold.

When the moon is at the full,
Mushrooms you may freely pull;
But when the moon is on the wane,
Wait ere you think to pluck again.

DIGGING

To-day I think
Only with scents, — scents dead leaves yield,
And bracken, and wild carrot's seed,
And the square mustard field;

Odours that rise
When the spade wounds the root of tree,
Rose, currant, raspberry, or goutweed,
Rhubarb or celery;

The smoke's smell, too,
Flowing from where a bonfire burns
The dead, the waste, the dangerous,
And all to sweetness turns.

It is enough
To smell, to crumble the dark earth,
While the robin sings over again
Sad songs of Autumn mirth.

    Edward Thomas (1878–1917)

October was well advanced, but steadily burning with a warmth that made the early months of the summer appear very young and capricious. Great tracts of the earth lay now beneath the autumn sun, and the whole of England, from the bald moors to the Cornish rocks, was lit up from dawn to sunset, and showed in stretches of yellow, green, and purple.

> Virginia Woolf (1882–1941), from *The Voyage Out*, 1915

A drizzling rain. Heavy masses of shapeless vapour upon the mountains (O the perpetual forms of Borrowdale!) yet it is no unbroken tale of dull sadness. Slanting pillars travel across the lake at long intervals, the vaporous mass whitens in large stains of light—on the lakeward ridge of that huge arm-chair of Lodore fell a gleam of softest light, that brought out the rich hues of the late autumn. The woody Castle Crag between me and Lodore is a rich flower-garden of colours—the brightest yellows with the deepest crimsons and the infinite shades of brown and green, the infinite diversity of which blends the whole, so that the brighter colours seem to be colours upon a ground, not coloured things. Little woolpacks of white bright vapour rest on different summits and declivities. The vale is narrowed by the mist and cloud, yet through the wall of mist you can see into a bower of sunny light, in Borrowdale; the birds are singing in the tender rain, as if it were the rain of April, and the decaying foliage were flowers and blossoms. The pillar of smoke from the chimney rises up in the mist, and is just distinguishable from it, and the mountain forms in the gorge of Borrowdale consubstantiate with the mist and cloud, even as the pillar'd smoke—a shade deeper and a determinate form.

> Samuel Taylor Coleridge (1772–1834), 21 October 1803

It was a very fine November day, and the Miss Musgroves came through the little grounds, and stopped for no other purpose than to say, that they were going to take a long walk, and, therefore, concluded Mary could not like to go with them; and when Mary immediately replied, with some jealousy at not being supposed a good walker, 'Oh, yes, I should like to join you very much, I am very fond of a long walk;' Anne felt persuaded, by the looks of the two girls, that it was precisely what they did not wish, and admired again the sort of necessity which the family habits seemed to produce, of everything being to be communicated, and everything being to be done together, however undesired and inconvenient. She tried to dissuade Mary from going, but in vain; and that being the case, thought it best to accept the Miss Musgroves' much more cordial invitation to herself to go likewise, as she might be useful in turning back with her sister, and lessening the interference in any plan of their own....

Anne's object was, not to be in the way of anybody; and where the narrow paths across the fields made many separations necessary, to keep with her brother and sister. Her pleasure in the walk must arise from the exercise and the day, from the view of the last smiles of the year upon the tawny leaves, and withered hedges, and from repeating to herself some few of the thousand poetical descriptions extant of autumn, that season of peculiar and inexhaustible influence on the mind of taste and tenderness, that season which had drawn from every poet, worthy of being read, some attempt at description, or some lines of feeling.

Jane Austen (1775–1817), from *Persuasion*, 1817

But the commonest bird, the one which vastly outnumbers all the others I have named together, is the starling. It was Caleb Bawcombe's favourite bird, and I believe it is regarded with peculiar affection by all shepherds on the downs on account of its constant association with sheep in the pasture. The dog, the sheep, and the crowd of starlings—these are the lonely man's companions during his long days on the hills from April or May to November. And what a wise bird he is, and how well he knows his friends and his enemies! There was nothing more beautiful to see, Caleb would say, than the behaviour of a flock of starlings when a hawk was about. If it was a kestrel they took little or no notice of it, but if a sparrowhawk made its appearance, instantly the crowd of birds could be seen flying at furious speed towards the nearest flock of sheep, and down into the flock they would fall like a shower of stones and instantly disappear from sight.

There they would remain on the ground, among the legs of the grazing sheep, until the hawk had gone on his way and passed out of sight.

W. H. Hudson (1841–1922), from *A Shepherd's Life*, 1910

The autumn drifted away through all its seasons. The golden corn-harvest, the walks through the stubble-fields, and rambles into hazel-copses in search of nuts; the stripping of the apple-orchards of their ruddy fruit, amid the joyous cries and shouts of watching children; and the gorgeous tulip-like colouring of the later time had now come on with the shortening days. There was comparative silence in the land, excepting for the distant shots, and the whirr of the partridges as they rose up from the field.

Elizabeth Gaskell (1810–1865), from *Wives and Daughters*, 1866

SEEING THE MOONLIGHT

Seeing the moonlight
spilling down
through these trees,
my heart fills to the brim
with autumn.

ONO NO KOMACHI (825—900 AD)

from THE BURNING OF THE LEAVES

Now is the time for the burning of the leaves.
They go to the fire; the nostril pricks with smoke
Wandering slowly into a weeping mist.
Brittle and blotched, ragged and rotten sheaves!
A flame seizes the smouldering ruin and bites
On stubborn stalks that crackle as they resist.

The last hollyhock's fallen tower is dust;
All the spices of June are a bitter reek,
All the extravagant riches spent and mean.
All burns! The reddest rose is a ghost;
Sparks whirl up, to expire in the mist: the wild
Fingers of fire are making corruption clean.

Now is the time for stripping the spirit bare,
Time for the burning of days ended and done,
Idle solace of things that have gone before:
Rootless hope and fruitless desire are there;
Let them go to the fire, with never a look behind.
The world that was ours is a world that is ours no more.

They will come again, the leaf and the flower, to arise
From squalor of rottenness into the old splendour,
And magical scents to a wondering memory bring;
The same glory, to shine upon different eyes.
Earth cares for her own ruins, naught for ours.
Nothing is certain, only the certain spring.

     Laurence Binyon (1869–1943)

Now November was upon us, and we had kept Allhallowmass, with roasting of skewered apples (like so many shuttlecocks), and after that the day of Fawkes… with merry bonfires and burned batatas.

R. D. Blackmore (1825–1900), from *Lorna Doone*, 1869

The evening might have been ordered with the fireworks; it was cold, still, and starry, with a commendable absence of moon. And when the first rocket went up Mrs. Miniver felt the customary pricking in her throat and knew that once again the enchantment was going to work. Some things—conjurers, ventriloquists, pantomimes—she enjoyed vicariously, by watching the children's enjoyment; but fireworks had for her a direct and magical appeal. Their attraction was more complex than that of any other form of art. They had pattern and sequence, colour and sound, brilliance and mobility; they had suspense, surprise, and a faint hint of danger; above all, they had the supreme quality of transience, which puts the keenest edge on beauty and makes it touch some spring in the heart which more enduring excellences cannot reach.

Jan Struther (1901–1953), from *Mrs Miniver*, 1939

The afternoon drew on apace, and, looking to the right towards the sea as he walked beside the horse, Poorgrass saw strange clouds and scrolls of mist rolling over the long ridges which girt the landscape in that quarter. They came in yet greater volumes, and indolently crept across the intervening valleys, and around the withered papery flags of the moor and river brinks. Then their dank spongy forms closed in upon the sky. It was a sudden overgrowth of atmospheric fungi which had their roots in the neighbouring sea, and by the time that horse, man, and corpse entered Yalbury Great Wood, these silent workings of an invisible hand had reached them, and they were completely enveloped, this being the first arrival of the autumn fogs, and the first fog of the series.

The air was as an eye suddenly struck blind. The waggon and its load rolled no longer on the horizontal division between clearness and opacity, but were imbedded in an elastic body of a monotonous pallor throughout. There was no perceptible motion in the air, not a visible drop of water fell upon a leaf of the beeches, birches, and firs composing the wood on either side. The trees stood in an attitude of intentness, as if they waited longingly for a wind to come and rock them. A startling quiet overhung all surrounding things — so completely, that the crunching of the waggon-wheels was as a great noise, and small rustles, which had never obtained a hearing except by night, were distinctly individualized.

Joseph Poorgrass looked round upon his sad burden as it loomed faintly through the flowering laurustinus, then at the unfathomable gloom amid the high trees on each hand, indistinct, shadowless, and spectre-like in their monochrome of grey. He felt anything but cheerful… The fog had by this time saturated the trees, and this was the first dropping of water from the overbrimming leaves. The hollow echo of its fall reminded the waggoner painfully of the grim Leveller. Then hard by came down another drop, then two or three. Presently there was a continual tapping of these heavy drops upon the dead leaves, the road, and the travellers. The nearer boughs were beaded with the mist to the greyness of aged men, and the rusty-red leaves of the beeches were hung with similar drops, like diamonds on auburn hair.

Thomas Hardy (1840–1928), from *Far from the Madding Crowd*, 1874

November—with uncanny witchery in its changed trees. With murky red sunsets flaming in smoky crimson behind the westering hills. With dear days when the austere woods were beautiful and gracious in a dignified serenity of folded hands and closed eyes—days full of a fine, pale sunshine that sifted through the late, leafless gold of the juniper-trees and glimmered among the grey beeches, lighting up evergreen banks of moss and washing the colonnades of the pines. Days with a high-sprung sky of flawless turquoise. Days when an exquisite melancholy seemed to hang over the landscape and dream about the lake. But days, too, of the wild blackness of great autumn storms, followed by dank, wet, streaming nights when there was witch-laughter in the pines and fitful moans among the mainland trees.

L. M. Montgomery (1874–1942), from *The Blue Castle*, 1926

How glad they all were when the long November day was over, and they could shut out the ceaseless drip-dripping of the rain, the sweep of the dead leaves across the windows! The autumn had been mild, and the foliage had lasted longer than usual. Now it came tumbling down with every breath, with every drop of rain, choking up the paths, and filling the air with the mournfullest downpouring of yellow. On such a day no one came up the avenue… and to look out upon the misty vista of the spectral trees, the damp rising from the ground and falling from the skies, both of which were about the same colour, for even a short November day is not cheerful to the spirits. It was a relief when the house began to be dotted with lamps, when the shutters were closed and the curtains drawn.

Margaret Oliphant (1828–1897), from *Mrs. Arthur*, 1877

AUTUMN FIRES

In the other gardens
And all up the vale,
From the autumn bonfires
See the smoke trail!

Pleasant summer over
And all the summer flowers,
The red fire blazes,
The grey smoke towers.

Sing a song of seasons!
Something bright in all!
Flowers in the summer,
Fires in the fall!

ROBERT LOUIS STEVENSON (1850—1894)

Books to read as the mist thickens

The Very Secret Society of Irregular Witches by Sangu Mandanna

*

O Caledonia by Elspeth Barker

*

Jane Eyre by Charlotte Brontë

*

The Thirteenth Tale by Diane Setterfield

*

The Little Stranger by Sarah Waters

*

The Woman in White by Wilkie Collins

from SUNSET WINGS

To-night this sunset spreads two golden wings
Cleaving the western sky;
Winged too with wind it is, and winnowings
Of birds; as if the day's last hour in rings
Of strenuous flight must die.

Sun-steeped in fire, the homeward pinions sway
Above the dovecote-tops;
And clouds of starlings, ere they rest with day,
Sink, clamorous like mill-waters, at wild play,
By turns in every copse:

Each tree heart-deep the wrangling rout receives,—
Save for the whirr within,
You could not tell the starlings from the leaves;
Then one great puff of wings, and the swarm heaves
Away with all its din.

DANTE GABRIEL ROSSETTI (1828—1882)

In the country even more than in the town it is best to be a hug-the-hearth during November. Except for a few rough-coated young stock the cattle and cart-horses have long ago been brought into stall and stable. All wild living things have sought shelter, many are already in a hibernating torpor.

The badger, with eyelids fast shut, is snugly asleep in his set under the green hill dreaming of succulent pig-nut roots; the hedgehog, rolled up in his leafy den, is in his fancy eagerly afoot after slugs and beetles… the doormouse, with his tail curled to touch his cold nose, sees in his quaint imagination hazel nuts more in number than he, with nimble forepaws, could have piled up in a lifetime of day-time reality.

Llewelyn Powys (1884–1939), from *The Twelve Months*, 1936

Autumn drew shiveringly to its end. One day something seemed to be gone from the gardens; the tenderer leaves of vegetables had shrunk under the first smart frost, and hung like faded linen rags; then the forest leaves, which had been descending at leisure, descended in haste and in multitudes, and all the golden colors that had hung overhead were now crowded together in a degraded mass underfoot, where the fallen myriads got redder and hornier, and curled themselves up to rot.

Thomas Hardy (1840–1928), from *The Woodlanders*, 1887

NOVEMBER

Now the last leaves are hanging on the trees,
And very few the flowers that glint along
The deep dark lanes and braes, erewhile as throng
With peeping posies as the limes with bees;
Nought in the garden but stiff sticks of peas,
And climbing weeds inextricably strong;
And scarce a fragment of autumnal song
Whistles above the surly morning breeze.
Yet still at eve we hear the merry owl,
That sings not sweetly, but he does his best;
The little brown bird with the scarlet vest
Chirrups away, though distant storms do howl.
Then let us not at dark November scowl,
But wait for Christmas with a cheerful breast.

Hartley Coleridge (1796–1849)

WINTER

Sweet blackbird is silenced with chaffinch and thrush,
Only wainscoated robin still chirps in the bush:
Soft sun-loving swallows have mustered in force,
And winged to the spice-teeming southlands their course.

Plump housekeeper dormouse has tucked himself neat,
Just a brown ball in moss with a morsel to eat:
Armed hedgehog has huddled him into the hedge,
While frogs scarce miss freezing deep down in the sedge.

Soft swallows have left us alone in the lurch,
But robin sits whistling to us from his perch:
If I were red robin, I'd pipe you a tune,
Would make you despise all the beauties of June.

But, since, that cannot be, let us draw round the fire,
Munch chestnuts, tell stories, and stir the blaze higher:
We'll comfort pinched robin with crumbs, little man,
Till he'll sing us the very best song that he can.

Christina Rossetti (1830–1894)

BEFORE THE ICE IS IN THE POOLS

Before the ice is in the pools—
Before the skaters go,
Or any check at nightfall
Is tarnished by the snow—
Before the fields have finished,
Before the Christmas tree,
Wonder upon wonder
Will arrive to me!

Emily Dickinson (1830–1886)

The pale beams of the waning moon still cast a shadow of the cottage, when the labourer rises from his heavy sleep on a winter's morning. Often he huddles on his things and slips his feet into his thick 'water-tights'—which are stiff and hard, having been wet over night—by no other light than this. If the household is comparatively well managed, however, he strikes a match, and his 'dip' shows at the window. But he generally prefers to save a candle, and clatters down the narrow steep stairs in the semi-darkness, takes a piece of bread and cheese, and steps forth into the sharp air. The cabbages in the garden he notes are covered with white frost, so is the grass in the fields, and the footpath is hard under foot. In the furrows is a little ice—white because the water has shrunk from beneath it, leaving it hollow—and on the stile is a crust of rime, cold to the touch, which he brushes off in getting over. Overhead the sky is clear—cloudless but pale—and the stars, though not yet fading, have lost the brilliant glitter of midnight. Then, in all their glory, the idea of their globular shape is easily accepted; but in the morning, just as the dawn is breaking, the absence of glitter comes the impression of flatness—circular rather than globular. But yonder, over the elms, above the cowpens, the great morning star has risen, shining far brighter, in proportion, than the moon; an intensely clear metallic light—like incandescent silver.

  Richard Jefferies (1848–1887), from *Hodge and His Masters*, 1880

Sleighs are out for the first time this winter; and, as usual, the good people enjoy the first sleighing extremely. Merry bells are jingling through the village streets; cutters and sleighs with gay parties dashing rapidly about.

  Susan Fenimore Cooper (1813–1894), from *Rural Hours*, 1850

It is warm in the cowshed; and if there is a more comfortable sound on a winter's morning than that of ten cows crunching a mixture of kale, chaff and oats, I have not heard it — unless it is that of horses feeding after a day at plough. It is a warm sound, mingled with the jingle of chains, and the occasional clank of our pails. It is warm against the cow's flank: milking lets you into the cold day's work gently. I like it; and the quiet, lamplit, rustling, munching row of bodies, and the sheer white walls and ceiling with the original cross-beams of the old shed adding a traditional touch to the cloistral bareness. It is one's morning orison to order, cleanliness, seemliness.

        Adrian Bell (1901–1980), from *The Budding Morrow*, 1946

A wren has found its way into my bedroom four mornings running. I have to open the double glazing to free it, feeling virtuous as the icy blasts rush at me. But, as William Blake rightly said, 'He who shall hurt the little wren / shall never be beloved of men.' And quite right too. One morning I caught the wren in my palms and carried it out into winter. It pulsated tenderly between my hands and was as warm as toast. And when I parted them in the garden, the tiny ex-prisoner hardly dared to take its freedom… For the winter's day cuts like a knife, so that even a wild bird hesitates to face it.

        Ronald Blythe (1922–2023), from *Borderland: Continuity and Change in the Countryside*, 2007

UP IN THE MORNING EARLY

Cauld blaws the wind frae east to west,
The drift is driving sairly;
Sae loud and shill's I hear the blast
I'm sure it's winter fairly.

Up in the morning's no for me,
Up in the morning early;
When a' the hills are covered wi' snaw,
I'm sure it's winter fairly.

The birds sit chittering in the thorn,
A' day they fare but sparely;
And lang's the night frae e'en to morn
I'm sure it's winter fairly.

Up in the morning's no for me,
Up in the morning early;
When a' the hills are covered wi' snaw,
I'm sure it's winter fairly.

Robert Burns (1759–1796)

from A NOCTURNAL UPON ST. LUCY'S DAY

The sun is spent, and now his flasks
Send forth light squibs, no constant rays;
　　The world's whole sap is sunk...

John Donne (1572–1631)

The first snowfall came early in December. I remember how the world looked from our sitting-room window as I dressed behind the stove that morning: the low sky was like a sheet of metal; the blond cornfields had faded out into ghostliness at last; the little pond was frozen under its stiff willow bushes. Big white flakes were whirling over everything and disappearing in the red grass…

It was a bright, cold day. I piled straw and buffalo robes into the box, and took two hot bricks wrapped in old blankets. When I got to the Shimerdas', I did not go up to the house, but sat in my sleigh at the bottom of the draw and called. Ántonia and Yulka came running out… They had heard about my sledge from Ambrosch and knew why I had come. They tumbled in beside me and we set off toward the north…

The sky was brilliantly blue, and the sunlight on the glittering white stretches of prairie was almost blinding. As Ántonia said, the whole world was changed by the snow; we kept looking in vain for familiar landmarks.

> Willa Cather (1873–1947), from *My Ántonia*, 1918

A pheasant trod delicately along the edge of the wood, and flew off with a gentle whirring of wings at our approach. A rabbit slipped through the bracken with a dull crackling sound and somewhere amongst the trees an owl began to hoot and then, finding it not quite dark yet, thought better of it, after all.

Again, at the entrance to the wood, on the lee side where the snow had not been able to drift so thickly, a solitary dead thistle was standing amongst the sheltering bushes — brown, withered, unlovely.

Yes, unlovely, yet not unwanted, for suddenly three bright unexpected goldfinches flew down the hedge and settled delicately on its dingy branches. Twisting and turning this way and that, they pecked a seed here and a seed there from the swaying thistle head, till the white down went floating away in all directions over the whiter snow. The every movement of these little birds was quick and fairylike, and now and then one of them would burst into a tiny little trill of song. Indeed, with their crimson caps, their black and white, and their yellow-barred wings against the spotless background of snow, they touched the withered plant into the most exquisite loveliness for a few fleeting moments.

Beryl Netherclift (1902–1986), from *Greensleeves*, 1939

At noon to-day I and my white greyhound, Mayflower, set out for a walk into a very beautiful world,—a sort of silent fairyland,—a creation of that matchless magician the hoar-frost. There had been just snow enough to cover the earth and all its covers with one sheet of pure and uniform white, and just time enough since the snow had fallen to allow the hedges to be freed of their fleecy load, and clothed with a delicate coating of rime. The atmosphere was deliciously calm; soft, even mild, in spite of the thermometer; no perceptible air, but a stillness that might almost be felt, the sky, rather gray than blue, throwing out in bold relief the snow-covered roofs of our village, and the rimy trees that rise above them, and the sun shining dimly as through a veil, giving a pale fair light, like the moon, only brighter. There was a silence, too, that might become the moon, as we stood at our little gate looking up the quiet street; a Sabbath-like pause of work and play, rare on a work-day; nothing was audible but the pleasant hum of frost, that low monotonous sound, which is perhaps the nearest approach that life and nature can make to absolute silence.

Mary Russell Mitford (1787–1855), from *Our Village*, 1824

from **ROBIN**

It's not so much that robins follow us
more like they lead the way, going on ahead
like useless guides with not one word of our
  language
but fluent in flow and lode, flitting along
whichever way we walk, breaking into song

before we catch up, and they're off again, a few
  yards
further into the future. We love them for this,
for spelling it out, for showing us where the edge
of the present moment is.

PAUL FARLEY (1965—)

SOME OF MY FAVOURITE COLLECTIVE NOUNS FOR BIRDS

A merl of blackbirds	A gaggle of geese
A worm of robins	A charm of goldfinches
A parliament of rooks	A glare of goshawks
A mischief of magpies	A prayer of godwits
A bellowing of bullfinches	A squabble of seagulls
An exultation of skylarks	A train of jackdaws
A confusion of chiffchaffs	A hover of kestrels
A wake of buzzards	An ascension of larks
A kettle of swallows	A wisdom of owls
A murder of crows	An ostentation of peacocks
An asylum of cuckoos	A conspiracy of ravens
A dole of doves	A quarrel of sparrows
A nye of pheasants	A murmuration of starlings
A paddling of ducks	A lamentation of swans
A trembling of finches	A chime of wrens
A scold of jays	A parcel of linnets

They went for long tramps through the exquisite reticence of winter woods and the silver jungles of frosted trees, and found loveliness everywhere.

At times they seemed to be walking through a spellbound world of crystal and pearl, so white and radiant were clearings and lakes and sky. The air was so crisp and clear that it was half intoxicating.

Once they stood in a hesitation of ecstasy at the entrance of a narrow path between ranks of birches. Every twig and spray was outlined in snow. The undergrowth along its sides was a little fairy forest cut out of marble. The shadows cast by the pale sunshine were fine and spiritual.

L. M. Montgomery (1874–1942), from The Blue Castle, 1926

They drove slowly up the road between fields glistening under the pale sun, and then bent to the right down a lane edged with spruce and larch. Ahead of them, a long way off, a range of hills stained by mottlings of black forest flowed away in round white curves against the sky. The lane passed into a pinewood with boles reddening in the afternoon sun and delicate blue shadows on the snow. As they entered it the breeze fell and a warm stillness seemed to drop from the branches with the dropping needles. Here the snow was so pure that the tiny tracks of wood animals had left on it intricate lace-like patterns, and the bluish cones caught in its surface stood out like ornaments of bronze.

Edith Wharton (1862–1937), from Ethan Frome, 1911

This radiant weather, when mere living is a joy, and sitting still over the fire out of the question, has been going on for more than a week. Sleighing and skating have been our chief occupation, especially skating, which is more than usually fascinating here, because the place is intersected by small canals communicating with a lake and the river belonging to the lake, and as everything is frozen black and hard, we can skate for miles straight ahead without being obliged to turn round and come back again, — at all times an annoying, and even mortifying, proceeding.... In some places the banks of the canals are so high that only our heads appear level with the fields, and it is... a curious sight to see three female heads skimming along apparently by themselves, and enjoying it tremendously. When the banks are low, we appear to be gliding deliciously over the roughest ploughed fields, with or without legs according to circumstances. Before we start, I fix on the place where tea and a sleigh are to meet us, and we drive home again; because skating against the wind is as detestable as skating with it is delightful, and an unkind Nature arranges its blowing without the smallest regard for our convenience.

Elizabeth von Arnim (1866–1941),
from *Elizabeth and Her German Garden*, 1898

Snow lay on the croft and river-bank in undulations softer than the limbs of infancy; it lay with the neatliest finished border on every sloping roof, making the dark-red gables stand out with a new depth of colour; it weighed heavily on the laurels and fir-trees, till it fell from them with a shuddering sound; it clothed the rough turnip-field with whiteness, and made the sheep look like dark blotches...

George Eliot (1819–1880), from *The Mill on the Floss*, 1860

from **THE WORLD OF TREES**
(inspired by the Forest of Burnley)

Sycamore. Mountain Ash. Beech. Birch. Oak.

The trees knew each other's secrets.
In the deep green heart of the forest.
Each tree loved another tree best.
Each tree, happy to rest, lean a little to the east,

or to the west, when the moon loomed high
   above,
the big white eye of the woods.
And they stood together as one in the dark,
with the stars sparkling from their branches,

completely at ease, breathing in the cold night
   air
swishing a little in the breeze,
dreaming of glossy spring leaves
in the fine, distinguished company of trees.

Jackie Kay (1961–)

FIRST KNOWN WHEN LOST

I never had noticed it until
'Twas gone, – the narrow copse
Where now the woodman lops
The last of the willows with his bill

It was not more than a hedge overgrown.
One meadow's breadth away
I passed it day by day.
Now the soil is bare as bone,

And black betwixt two meadows green,
Though fresh-cut faggot ends
Of hazel made some amends
With a gleam as if flowers they had been.

Strange it could have hidden so near!
And now I see as I look
That the small winding brook,
A tributary's tributary, rises there.

EDWARD THOMAS (1878—1917)

A WINTER BLUE JAY

Crisply the bright snow whispered,
Crunching beneath our feet;
Behind us as we walked along the parkway,
Our shadows danced,
Fantastic shapes in vivid blue.
Across the lake the skaters
Flew to and fro,
With sharp turns weaving
A frail invisible net.
In ecstasy the earth
Drank the silver sunlight;
In ecstasy the skaters
Drank the wine of speed;
In ecstasy we laughed
Drinking the wine of love.
Had not the music of our joy
Sounded its highest note?

But no,
For suddenly, with lifted eyes you said,
'Oh look!'
There, on the black bough of a snow flecked maple,
Fearless and gay as our love,
A bluejay cocked his crest!
Oh who can tell the range of joy
Or set the bounds of beauty?

Sara Teasdale (1884–1933)

WINTER
Country Contentments

The first snowfall.

Rosy cheeks, flushed from the cold.

Gleaming bottles of sloe gin brought
out from the larder.

A lighted candle flickering in the window.

Watching the breathtaking spectacle of a starling
murmuration.

Toasting fingers and toes by the fire.

An owl's haunting call piercing the nighttime stillness.

Fairy frost patterns on the greenhouse glass.

The trill of a robin in the holly tree.

Looking up at the star-pricked sky
on a clear, frosty night.

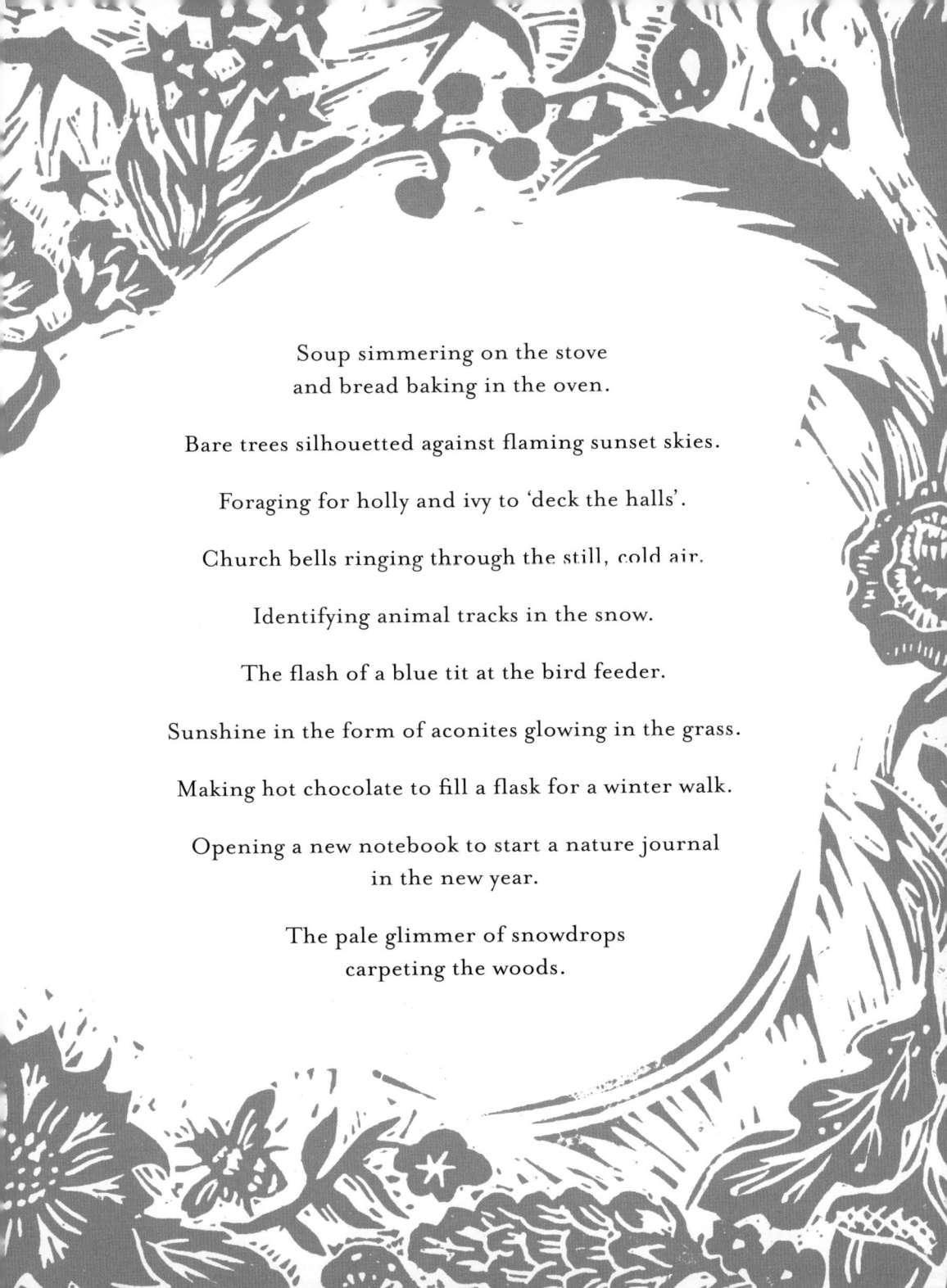

Soup simmering on the stove
and bread baking in the oven.

Bare trees silhouetted against flaming sunset skies.

Foraging for holly and ivy to 'deck the halls'.

Church bells ringing through the still, cold air.

Identifying animal tracks in the snow.

The flash of a blue tit at the bird feeder.

Sunshine in the form of aconites glowing in the grass.

Making hot chocolate to fill a flask for a winter walk.

Opening a new notebook to start a nature journal
in the new year.

The pale glimmer of snowdrops
carpeting the woods.

from THE PRELUDE

And in the frosty season, when the sun
Was set, and visible for many a mile
The cottage windows through the twilight blaz'd,
I heeded not the summons:—happy time
It was, indeed, for all of us; to me
It was a time of rapture: clear and loud
The village clock toll'd six; I wheel'd about,
Proud and exulting, like an untired horse,
That cares not for its home.—All shod with steel,
We hiss'd along the polish'd ice, in games
Confederate, imitative of the chase
And woodland pleasures, the resounding horn,
The Pack loud bellowing, and the hunted hare.
So through the darkness and the cold we flew,
And not a voice was idle; with the din,
Meanwhile, the precipices rang aloud,
The leafless trees, and every icy crag
Tinkled like iron, while the distant hills
Into the tumult sent an alien sound
Of melancholy, not unnoticed, while the stars,
Eastward, were sparkling clear, and in the west
The orange sky of evening died away.

William Wordsworth (1770–1850)

Winter Tea

It is mid-winter, dark December. It is Sunday afternoon. In boots and greatcoats, mufflers and mittens, everyone has gone for a walk, except perhaps for grandmama and great-aunt, who snooze beside the fire, and the cats, stretched sleek on the hearthrug.

They have gone across the fields towards the wood. The air is damp, raw, cold, it catches the breath. Early this morning, and late tonight, comes the frost, hardening the earth….

The children are tumbling and gambolling and racing in zig-zags, voices carrying on the still, chill air. Stamping of feet, blowing on fingers, beating of arms.

And now the sun sets, rose-red and blazing, below the hill.

Bones ache, teeth chatter, skin chaps, noses run. They are heading for home, and, in the house ahead, the lamps come on in welcome, and the clock stirs, gathers itself, then chimes.

It is time for tea.

Susan Hill (1942–), from *Through the Kitchen Window*, 1984

I once gave a lady two-and-twenty recipes against melancholy: one was a bright fire; another, to remember all the pleasant things said to and of her; another, to keep a box of sugar-plums on the chimneypiece, and a kettle simmering on the hob. I thought this mere trifling at the moment, but have in after-life discovered how true it is that these little pleasures often banish melancholy better than higher and more exalted objects; and that no means ought to be thought too trifling which can oppose it either in ourselves or others.

Sydney Smith (1771–1845), from *Memoir of the Rev. Sydney Smith*, 1874

THE FIREWOOD POEM

Beechwood fires are bright and clear
If the logs are kept a year,
Chestnut's only good they say,
If for logs 'tis laid away.
Make a fire of Elder tree,
Death within your house will be;
But ash new or ash old,
Is fit for a queen with crown of gold

Birch and fir logs burn too fast
Blaze up bright and do not last,
it is by the Irish said
Hawthorn bakes the sweetest bread.
Elm wood burns like churchyard mould,
E'en the very flames are cold
But ash green or ash brown
Is fit for a queen with golden crown

Poplar gives a bitter smoke,
Fills your eyes and makes you choke,
Apple wood will scent your room
Pear wood smells like flowers in bloom
Oaken logs, if dry and old
keep away the winter's cold
But ash wet or ash dry
a king shall warm his slippers by.

                    Celia Congreve (1867–1952)

There is something in the very season of the year that gives a charm to the festivity of Christmas. At other times we derive a great portion of our pleasures from the mere beauties of nature. Our feelings sally forth and dissipate themselves over the sunny landscape, and we 'live abroad and everywhere.' The song of the bird, the murmur of the stream, the breathing fragrance of spring, the soft voluptuousness of summer, the golden pomp of autumn; earth with its mantle of refreshing green, and heaven with its deep delicious blue and its cloudy magnificence, all fill us with mute but exquisite delight, and we revel in the luxury of mere sensation. But in the depth of winter, when nature lies despoiled of every charm, and wrapped in her shroud of sheeted snow, we turn for our gratifications to moral sources. The dreariness and desolation of the landscape, the short gloomy days and darksome nights, while they circumscribe our wanderings, shut in our feelings also from rambling abroad, and make us more keenly disposed for the pleasures of the social circle. Our thoughts are more concentrated; our friendly sympathies more aroused, we feel more sensibly the charm of each other's society, and are brought more closely together by dependence on each other for enjoyment. Heart calleth unto heart; and we draw our pleasures from the deep wells of living kindness, which lie in the quiet recesses of our bosoms: and which when resorted to, furnish forth the pure element of domestic felicity.

  Washington Irving (1783–1859), from *Old Christmas*, 1876

Fine old Christmas, with the snowy hair and ruddy face, had done his duty that year in the noblest fashion, and had set off his rich gifts of warmth and colour with all the heightening contrast of frost and snow.

  George Eliot (1819–1880), from *The Mill on the Floss*, 1860

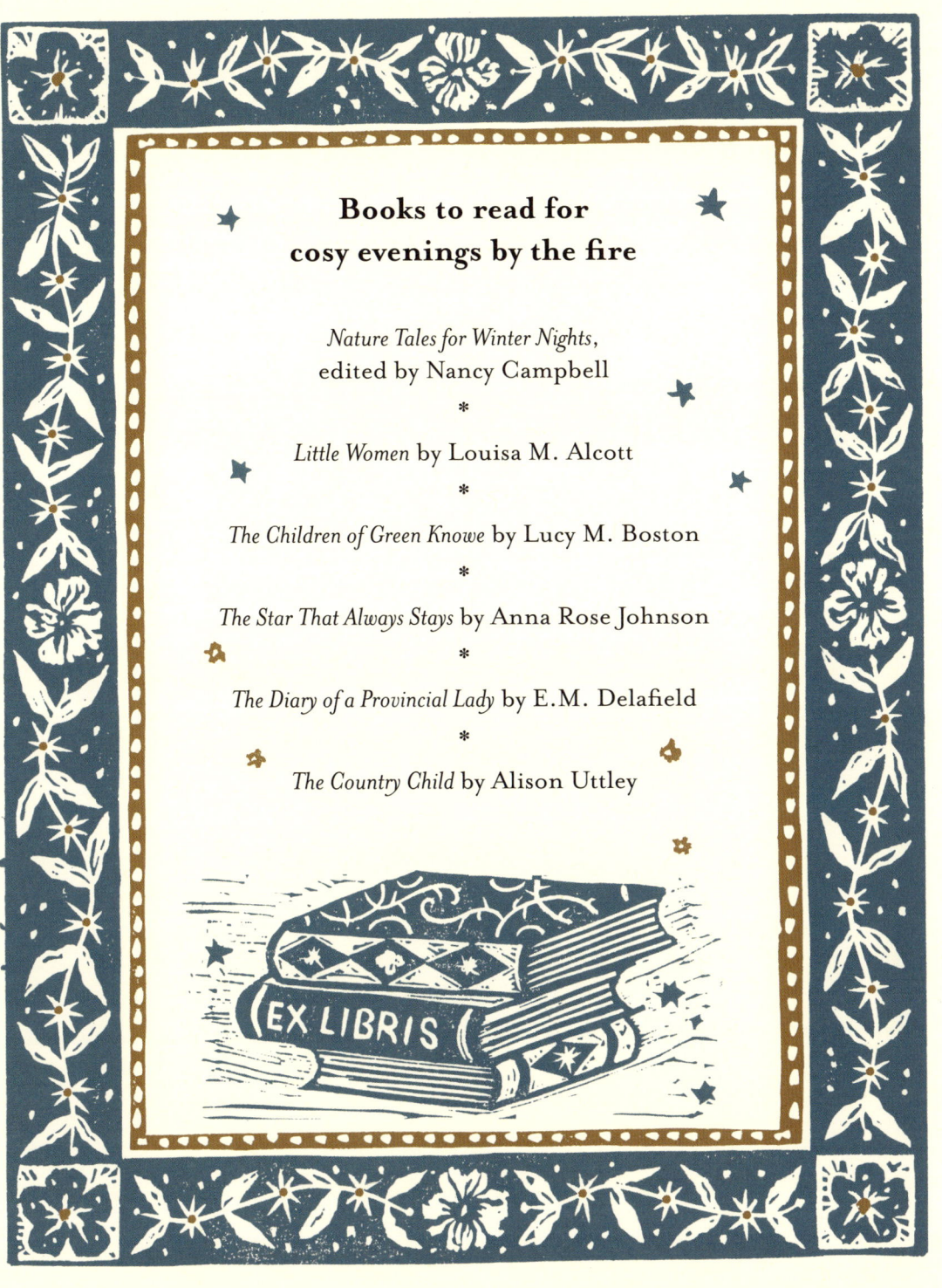

Books to read for cosy evenings by the fire

Nature Tales for Winter Nights,
edited by Nancy Campbell

*

Little Women by Louisa M. Alcott

*

The Children of Green Knowe by Lucy M. Boston

*

The Star That Always Stays by Anna Rose Johnson

*

The Diary of a Provincial Lady by E.M. Delafield

*

The Country Child by Alison Uttley

WINTER GLÖGG

A warming and fragrant winter drink, especially popular at Christmas.

Makes 6–8 glasses

INGREDIENTS

500ml (17fl oz) red wine (Merlot or Malbec work well)

Peel of 2 oranges

30g (1oz) whole, skinned almonds

30g (1oz) raisins

2 sticks of cinnamon

3cm (1 inch) piece of peeled, fresh ginger, sliced

125g (4½oz) caster sugar

4 cloves

5 cardamom pods

150ml (5¼fl oz) vodka

100ml (3½fl oz) white rum

METHOD

1. Place all of the ingredients, except the vodka and the rum, into a large saucepan and warm gently over a medium heat, stirring until all the sugar has dissolved completely. Be careful not to boil.

2. Using a slotted spoon, remove the raisins and almonds from the liquid and divide between six to eight glasses, depending on their size.

3. Strain the hot liquid through a sieve set over a large heatproof jug.

4. Stir in the vodka and rum.

5. Divide the red wine mixture between the glasses and have small teaspoons available, as required, so guests can eat the raisins and almonds in the drained glasses too.

CHRISTMAS CAROL

Dress the walls with casuarina,
Flaming red poinsettia too,
Mix among them allamanda,
Hibiscus of countless hues,
Snow-on-the-mountain, poinciana,
Christmas candles 'cross the door.
Pink and purple bougainvillea,
For it's Christmas-time once more.

Pick the sorrel from the stalk now,
It's that special time of year,
Reap the swollen ginger root and
Make the special ginger beer,
Tangerines are ripe and juicy,
Sweet oranges by the score,
Dig the yams, they'll now be ready,
For it's Christmas-time once more.

Valerie Bloom (1956–)

THE OXEN

Christmas Eve, and twelve of the clock.
'Now they are all on their knees,'
An elder said as we sat in a flock
By the embers in hearthside ease.

We pictured the meek mild creatures where
They dwelt in their strawy pen,
Nor did it occur to one of us there
To doubt they were kneeling then.

So fair a fancy few would weave
In these years! Yet, I feel,
If someone said on Christmas Eve,
'Come; see the oxen kneel,

'In the lonely barton by yonder coomb
Our childhood used to know,'
I should go with him in the gloom,
Hoping it might be so.

THOMAS HARDY (1840—1928)

Gradually there gathered the feeling of expectation. Christmas was coming. In the shed, at nights, a secret candle was burning, a sound of veiled voices was heard... Twice a week, by lamplight, there was choir practice in the church, for the learning of old carols Brangwen wanted to hear. The girls went to these practices. Everywhere was a sense of mystery and rousedness. Everybody was preparing for something.

    The time came near, the girls were decorating the church, with cold fingers binding holly and fir and yew about the pillars, till a new spirit was in the church, the stone broke out into dark, rich leaf, the arches put forth their buds, and cold flowers rose to blossom in the dim, mystic atmosphere. Ursula must weave mistletoe over the door, and over the screen, and hang a silver dove from a sprig of yew, till dusk came down, and the church was like a grove....

                  D. H. Lawrence (1885–1930), from *The Rainbow*, 1915

It was a pretty sight, and a seasonable one, that met their eyes when they flung the door open. In the fore-court, lit by the dim rays of a horn lantern, some eight or ten little field-mice stood in a semi-circle, red worsted comforters round their throats, their fore-paws thrust deep into their pockets, their feet jigging for warmth. With bright beady eyes they glanced shyly at each other, sniggering a little, sniffing and applying coat-sleeves a good deal. As the door opened, one of the elder ones that carried the lantern was just saying, 'Now then, one, two, three!' and forthwith their shrill little voices uprose in the air, singing one of the old-time carols that their forefathers composed in fields that were fallow and held by frost, or when snow-bound in chimney corners, and handed down to be sung in the miry street to lamp-lit windows at Yule-time.

                Kenneth Grahame (1859–1932), from *The Wind in the Willows*, 1908

From the centre of the ceiling of this kitchen, old Wardle had just suspended, with his own hands, a huge branch of mistletoe, and this same branch of mistletoe instantaneously gave rise to a scene of general and most delightful struggling and confusion; in the midst of which, Mr. Pickwick, with a gallantry that would have done honour to a descendant of Lady Tollimglower herself, took the old lady by the hand, led her beneath the mystic branch, and saluted her in all courtesy and decorum. The old lady submitted to this piece of practical politeness with all the dignity which befitted so important and serious a solemnity, but the younger ladies, not being so thoroughly imbued with a superstitious veneration for the custom, or imagining that the value of a salute is very much enhanced if it cost a little trouble to obtain it, screamed and struggled, and ran into corners, and threatened and remonstrated, and did everything but leave the room, until some of the less adventurous gentlemen were on the point of desisting, when they all at once found it useless to resist any longer, and submitted to be kissed with a good grace….

Now, the screaming had subsided, and faces were in a glow, and curls in a tangle, and Mr. Pickwick… was standing under the mistletoe, looking with a very pleased countenance on all that was passing around him, when the young lady with the black eyes, after a little whispering with the other young ladies, made a sudden dart forward, and, putting her arm round Mr. Pickwick's neck, saluted him affectionately on the left cheek; and before Mr. Pickwick distinctly knew what was the matter, he was surrounded by the whole body, and kissed by every one of them.

It was a pleasant thing to see Mr. Pickwick in the centre of the group, now pulled this way, and then that, and first kissed on the chin, and then on the nose, and then on the spectacles, and to hear the peals of laughter which were raised on every side; but it was a still more pleasant thing to see Mr. Pickwick, blinded shortly afterwards with a silk handkerchief, falling up against the wall, and scrambling into corners, and going through all the mysteries of blind-man's buff, with the utmost relish for the game, until at last he caught one of the poor relations, and then had to evade the blind-man himself, which he did with a nimbleness and agility that elicited the admiration and applause of all beholders. The poor relations caught the people who they thought would like it, and, when the game flagged, got caught themselves. When they all tired of blind-man's buff, there was a great game at snap-dragon, and when fingers enough were burned with that, and all the raisins were gone, they sat down by the huge fire of blazing logs to a substantial supper, and a mighty bowl of wassail, something smaller than an ordinary wash-house copper, in which the hot apples were hissing and bubbling with a rich look, and a jolly sound, that were perfectly irresistible.

'This,' said Mr. Pickwick, looking round him, 'this is, indeed, comfort.' 'Our invariable custom,' replied Mr. Wardle. 'Everybody sits down with us on Christmas Eve, as you see them now — servants and all; and here we wait, until the clock strikes twelve, to usher Christmas in, and beguile the time with forfeits and old stories. Trundle, my boy, rake up the fire.'

Up flew the bright sparks in myriads as the logs were stirred. The deep red blaze sent forth a rich glow, that penetrated into the farthest corner of the room, and cast its cheerful tint on every face.

Charles Dickens (1812–1870), from *The Pickwick Papers*, 1837

'Christmas weather,' observed Mr. Elton. 'Quite seasonable; and extremely fortunate we may think ourselves that it did not begin yesterday, and prevent this day's party, which it might very possibly have done, for Mr. Woodhouse would hardly have ventured had there been much snow on the ground; but now it is of no consequence. This is quite the season indeed for friendly meetings. At Christmas every body invites their friends about them, and people think little of even the worst weather. I was snowed up at a friend's house once for a week. Nothing could be pleasanter. I went for only one night, and could not get away till that very day se'nnight.'

    Mr. John Knightley looked as if he did not comprehend the pleasure....

Jane Austen (1775–1817), from *Emma*, 1815

In the middle of the table was a Christmas tree, alive and growing, looking very much surprised at itself, for had not Tom dug it up... whilst they were at church, and brought it in with real snow on its branches? The rosiest of apples and the nicest yellow oranges were strung to its boughs, and some sugar biscuits with pink icing and a few humbugs from Tom's pocket lay on the snow, with a couple gaily coloured texts and a sugar elephant. On the top of the tree shone a silver bird, a most astonishing silver glass peacock with a tail of fine feathers, which might have flown in at the window....

Alison Uttley (1884–1976), from *The Country Child*, 1931

THE CHRISTMAS LIFE

'If you don't have a real tree you don't bring the Christmas life into the house.' Josephine Mackinnon, aged 8

Bring in a tree, a young Norwegian spruce,
Bring hyacinths that rooted in the cold.
Bring winter jasmine as its buds unfold –
Bring the Christmas life into this house.

Bring red and green and gold, bring things that shine,
Bring candlesticks and music, food and wine.
Bring in your memories of Christmas past.
Bring in your tears for all that you have lost.

Bring in the shepherd boy, the ox and ass,
Bring in the stillness of an icy night,
Bring in the birth, of hope and love and light.
Bring the Christmas life into this house.

Wendy Cope (1945–)

from DECEMBER
(THE SHEPHERD'S CALENDAR)

Glad Christmas comes, and every hearth
    Makes room to give him welcome now,
E'en want will dry its tears in mirth,
    And crown him with a holly bough;
Though tramping 'neath a winter sky,
    O'er snowy paths and rimy stiles,
The housewife sets her spinning by
    To bid him welcome with her smiles.

Each house is swept the day before,
    And windows stuck with ever-greens,
The snow is besom'd from the door,
    And comfort crowns the cottage scenes.
Gilt holly, with its thorny pricks,
    And yew and box, with berries small,
These deck the unused candlesticks,
    And pictures hanging by the wall.

Neighbours resume their annual cheer,
   Wishing, with smiles and spirits high,
Glad Christmas and a happy new year,
   To every morning passer-by;
Milkmaids their Christmas journeys go,
   Accompanied with favour'd swain;
And children pace the crumping snow,
   To taste their granny's cake again.

John Clare (1793–1864)

WINTER TRADITIONAL COUNTRY WISDOM

Red sky at night, shepherd's delight,
Red sky in the morning, shepherd's warning.

If Christmas Day on Thursday be,
A windy winter you shall see,
Windy weather in each week,
And hard tempests strong and thick,
The summer shall be good and dry,
Corn and beasts shall multiply.

Bees sing in their hives on Christmas Eve.

When the sun shines through
apple boughs on Christmas Day,
there's bound to be a good crop.

If the robin sings in the bush
Then the weather will be coarse;
But if the robin sings in the barn,
Then the weather will be warm.

If Candlemas day be sunny and bright
Winter will have another flight.
But if Candlemas day be clouds and rain,
Winter is gone and will not come again.

A leap year is never a good sheep year.

I HEARD A BIRD SING

I heard a bird sing
In the dark of December.
A magical thing
And sweet to remember.

'We are nearer to Spring
Than we were in September,'
I heard a bird sing
In the dark of December.

Oliver Herford (1860–1935)

ANOTHER CHRISTMAS GONE

The first white hill still glistens
Beneath the moonlit skies;
As on the night of Christmas
Untrod it sleeping lies,
A new born year is waiting
To meet the early dawn:
And whisper this to all the world,
Another Christmas gone.

Anonymous

RING OUT, WILD BELLS
from **IN MEMORIAM**

Ring out, wild bells, to the wild sky,
  The flying cloud, the frosty light:
  The year is dying in the night;
Ring out, wild bells, and let him die.

Ring out the old, ring in the new,
  Ring, happy bells, across the snow:
  The year is going, let him go;
Ring out the false, ring in the true.

ALFRED, LORD TENNYSON (1809—1892)

Wassail-bowl, a centre Supper Dish for Christmastide.— Crumble down as for trifle a fresh rice-cake (or use macaroons or other small biscuit) into a china punch-bowl or deep glass dish. Over this pour some sweet, rich wine, as Malmsey Madeira, if wanted very rich, but raisin-wine will do. Sweeten this, and pour a high-seasoned rich custard over it. Strew nutmeg and grated sugar lightly over it, and ornament it with sliced blanched almonds.— Obs. This is, in fact, just a rich eating posset, or the more modern Tipsy-Cake.... A very good wassail-bowl may be made with mild ale, well spiced or sweetened, and a plain custard made with few eggs. The wassail-bowl was anciently crowned with garlands and ribbons, and ushered in with carols and songs,— a custom worthy of revival.

Margaret Dods, pseudonym of Christian Isobel Johnstone (1781–1857), from *The Cook and Housewife's Manual*, 1826

Twelfth Night Wassailing Song

Here's to thee, old apple tree!
Whence thou may'st bud and whence thou may'st blow
And whence thou may'st have apples enow!
Hats full! Caps full!
Bushel—bushel—sacks full,
And my pockets full too! Huzza!

Traditional

SAINT DISTAFF'S DAY, OR THE MORROW AFTER TWELFTH DAY

Partly work and partly play
Ye must on S. Distaff's day:
From the plough soon free your team,
Then come home and fodder them.
If the maids a-spinning go,
Burn the flax and fire the tow;
Scorch their plackets, but beware
That ye singe no maidenhair.
Bring in pails of water, then,
Let the maids bewash the men.
Give S. Distaff all the right,
Then bid Christmas sport good-night;
And next morrow everyone
To his own vocation.

Robert Herrick (1591–1674)

It is January, and the predominant grass is green and shining in the sun. The rusty oaks and the farmhouse roofs glow. The bare clean hedges glitter with all their stems of olive hazel, silver oak and ash and white thorn, and blackthorn ruddy where the cattle have rubbed. A lark rises and sings. A flock of linnets scatters and drops little notes like a rain of singing dew, and over all is a high blue sky, across which the west wind sets a fleet of bright white clouds to sail; into this blue sky the woods of the horizon drive their black teeth.

> Edward Thomas (1878–1917), from *The Heart of England*, 1906

The ground was hard, the air was still, my road was lonely; I walked fast till I got warm, and then I walked slowly to enjoy and analyse the species of pleasure brooding for me in the hour and situation. It was three o'clock; the church bell tolled as I passed under the belfry: the charm of the hour lay in its approaching dimness, in the low-gliding and pale-beaming sun. I was a mile from Thornfield, in a lane noted for wild roses in summer, for nuts and blackberries in autumn, and even now possessing a few coral treasures in hips and haws, but whose best winter delight lay in its utter solitude and leafless repose. If a breath of air stirred, it made no sound here; for there was not a holly, not an evergreen to rustle, and the stripped hawthorn and hazel bushes were as still as the white, worn stones which causewayed the middle of the path. Far and wide, on each side, there were only fields, where no cattle now browsed; and the little brown birds, which stirred occasionally in the hedge, looked like single russet leaves that had forgotten to drop.

> Charlotte Brontë (1816–1855), from *Jane Eyre*, 1847

from ON HEARING A SMALL BIRD SING IN THE WINTER

Pretty little sprightly thing,
That so charming canst sing:
Tho' the rough wind keenly blow,
Bringing rain, or hail, or snow.

Lovely songster! sing again,
Whistle loud thy trilling strain;
Winter soon will pass away,
With his short and gloomy day.

Earnest of the genial year,
Soon the snowdrops shall appear;
Soon the primrose too shall shew
To the eye its lovely hue.

Thomas Shoel (1759–1823)

Books for the country diarist

Claxton by Mark Cocker

✻

The Country Diary of an Edwardian Lady by Edith Holden

✻

Diary of Country Parson, 1758–1802 by James Woodforde

✻

Kilvert's Diary by the Reverend Francis Kilvert

✻

All Around the Year by Michael Morpurgo

✻

Notes from Walnut Tree Farm by Roger Deakin

When I came out the night was superb. The sky was cloudless, the moon rode high and full in the deep blue vault and the evening star blazed in the west. The air was filled with the tolling and chiming of bells from St Paul's and Chippenham old Church. The night was soft and still and I walked up and down the drive several times before I could make up my mind to leave the wonderful beauty of the night and go indoors. To be alone out of doors on a still soft clear moonlit night is to me one of the greatest pleasures that this world can give.

    The Reverend Francis Kilvert (1840–1879), Sunday 12 January 1873

January 25th.— Attend a Committee Meeting in the village to discuss how to raise funds for Village Hall. Am asked to take the chair. Begin by saying that I know how much we all have this excellent object at heart, and that I feel sure there will be no lack of suggestions as to best method of obtaining requisite sum of money. Pause for suggestions, which is met with death-like silence. I say, There are so many ways to choose from — implication being that I attribute silence to plethora of ideas, rather than to absence of them. (*Note*: Curious and rather depressing, to see how frequently the pursuit of Good Works leads to apparently unavoidable duplicity.) Silence continues, and I say Well, twice, and Come, come, once. (Sudden impulse to exclaim, 'I lift up my finger and I say Tweet, Tweet,' is fortunately overcome.)

    E. M. Delafield (1890–1943), from *The Diary of a Provincial Lady*, 1930

January is when the chimney moans as south-westerly gales howl through the trees and hammer at our door. It is the month of brief, crimped days when the dogs won't stir from their baskets; the month of thick gloves, neck-hugging scarves and fur hats, of tightly drawn curtains and glowing firesides; it is the month of hunkering down and staying put.

John Lister-Kaye (1946–), from *Gods of the Morning*, 2016

The Great Frost was, historians tell us, the most severe that has ever visited these islands. Birds froze in mid-air and fell like stones to the ground. At Norwich a young countrywoman started to cross the road in her usual robust health and was seen by the onlookers to turn visibly to powder and be blown in a puff of dust over the roofs as the icy blast struck her at the street corner. The mortality among sheep and cattle was enormous. Corpses froze and could not be drawn from the sheets. It was no uncommon sight to come upon a whole herd of swine frozen immovable upon the road. The fields were full of shepherds, ploughmen, teams of horses, and little bird-scaring boys all struck stark in the act of the moment, one with his hand to his nose, another with the bottle to his lips, a third with a stone raised to throw at the raven who sat, as if stuffed, upon the hedge within a yard of him. The severity of the frost was so extraordinary that a kind of petrifaction sometimes ensued; and it was commonly supposed that the great increase of rocks in some parts of Derbyshire was due to no eruption, for there was none, but to the solidification of unfortunate wayfarers who had been turned literally to stone where they stood.

Virginia Woolf (1882–1941), from *Orlando*, 1928

from JANUARY

Cold is the winter day, misty and dark:
The sunless sky with faded gleams is rent:
And patches of thin snow outlying, mark
The landscape with a drear disfigurement.

The trees their mournful branches lift aloft:
The oak with knotty twigs is full of trust,
With bud-thronged bough the cherry in the croft;
The chestnut holds her gluey knops upthrust.

No birds sing, but the starling chaps his bill
And chatters mockingly; the newborn lambs
Within their strawbuilt fold beneath the hill
Answer with plaintive cry their bleating dams.

Their voices melt in welcome dreams of spring,
Green grass and leafy trees and sunny skies:
My fancy decks the woods, the thrushes sing,
Meadows are gay, bees hum and scents arise.

ROBERT BRIDGES (1844—1930)

from **THE SNOW STORM**

Announced by all the trumpets of the sky,
Arrives the snow, and, driving o'er the fields,
Seems nowhere to alight: the whited air
Hides hills and woods, the river, and the heaven,
And veils the farm-house at the garden's end.
The sled and traveler stopped, the courier's feet
Delayed, all friends shut out, the housemates sit
Around the radiant fireplace, enclosed
In a tumultuous privacy of storm.

    Ralph Waldo Emerson (1803–1882)

WINTER
from LOVE'S LABOUR'S LOST, ACT V, SCENE II

When icicles hang by the wall,
    And Dick the shepherd blows his nail,
And Tom bears logs into the hall,
    And milk comes frozen home in pail,
When blood is nipp'd and ways be foul,
Then nightly sings the staring owl,
            Tu-whit!
Tu-who! — a merry note,
While greasy Joan doth keel the pot.

When all aloud the wind doth blow,
    And coughing drowns the parson's saw,
And birds sit brooding in the snow,
    And Marian's nose looks red and raw,
When roasted crabs hiss in the bowl,
Then nightly sings the staring owl,
            Tu-whit!
Tu-who! — a merry note,
While greasy Joan doth keel the pot.

WILLIAM SHAKESPEARE (1564—1616)

That great snow never ceased a moment for three days and nights; and then when all the earth was filled, and the topmost hedges were unseen, and the trees broke down with weight (wherever the wind had not lightened them), a brilliant sun broke forth and showed the loss of all our customs.

All our house was quite snowed up, except where we had purged a way, by dint of constant shovellings. The kitchen was as dark and darker than the cider-cellar, and long lines of furrowed scollops ran even up to the chimney-stacks. Several windows fell right inwards, through the weight of the snow against them; and the few that stood, bulged in, and bent like an old bruised lanthorn. We were obliged to cook by candle-light; we were forced to read by candle-light; as for baking, we could not do it, because the oven was too chill; and a load of faggots only brought a little wet down the sides of it.

For when the sun burst forth at last upon that world of white, what he brought was neither warmth, nor cheer, nor hope of softening; only a clearer shaft of cold, from the violet depths of sky. Long-drawn alleys of white haze seemed to lead towards him, yet such as he could not come down, with any warmth remaining. Broad white curtains of the frost-fog looped around the lower sky, on the verge of hill and valley, and above the laden trees. Only round the sun himself, and the spot of heaven he claimed, clustered a bright purple-blue, clear, and calm, and deep.

That night such a frost ensued as we had never dreamed of, neither read in ancient books, or histories of Frobisher. The kettle by the fire froze, and the crock upon the hearth-cheeks; many men were killed, and cattle rigid in their head-ropes. Then I heard that fearful sound, which never I had heard before, neither since have heard (except during that same winter), the sharp yet solemn sound of trees burst open by the frost-blow.

R. D. Blackmore (1825–1900), from *Lorna Doone*, 1869

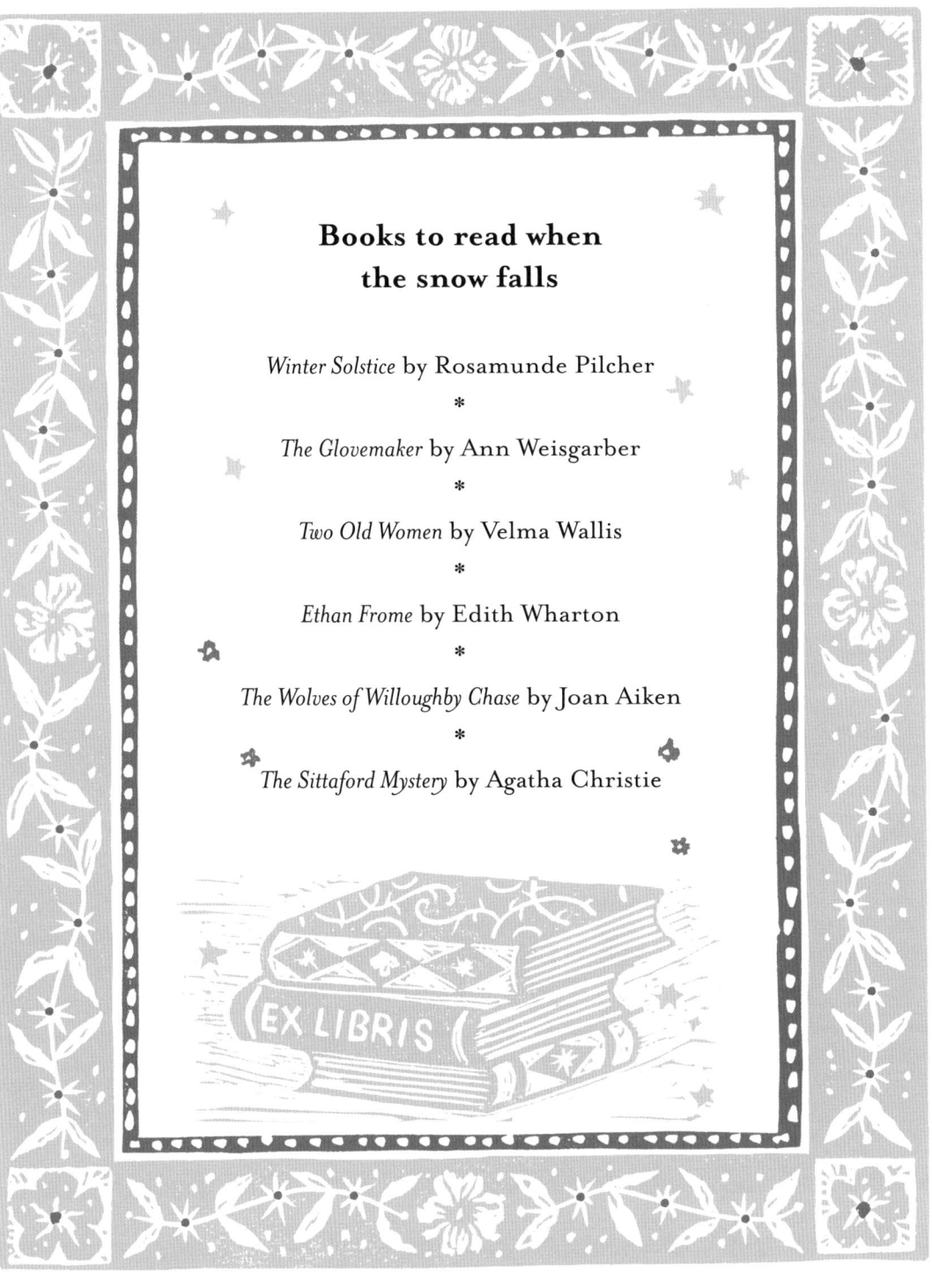

Books to read when the snow falls

Winter Solstice by Rosamunde Pilcher

*

The Glovemaker by Ann Weisgarber

*

Two Old Women by Velma Wallis

*

Ethan Frome by Edith Wharton

*

The Wolves of Willoughby Chase by Joan Aiken

*

The Sittaford Mystery by Agatha Christie

BLOOD ORANGE DRIZZLE CAKE

A comforting cake, full of fresh citrus flavour that's welcome in late winter.

Makes 1 large cake; serves 8

INGREDIENTS

175g (6oz) butter, softened

175g (6oz) golden caster sugar

3 large eggs, at room temperature

175g (6oz) self-raising flour, sifted

Finely grated zest of 1 blood orange

25ml (¾fl oz) freshly squeezed blood orange juice

2 tsps Grand Marnier or Orange Brandy or an additional 2 tsps of blood orange juice (optional)

For the drizzle

100ml (3½fl oz) freshly squeezed blood orange juice

100g (3½oz) golden caster sugar

This cake keeps well for 3 to 4 days, covered in foil and parchment wrap and stored in an airtight container.

METHOD

1. Preheat the oven to 180°C (160°C Fan), 350°F, Gas Mark 4. Grease and base line a 23cm (9 inch) round cake tin.
2. Cream together the softened butter and caster sugar with a handheld mixer in a large mixing bowl until pale and fluffy.
3. Beat in the eggs, one at a time, until the mixture is well combined.
4. Gently fold in the sifted self-raising flour, grated blood orange zest, juice and alcohol (if using) with a large metal spoon until all is well combined.
5. Spoon into the prepared cake tin and level the top.
6. Bake in the preheated oven for 30–35 minutes, or until the cake is lightly browned and a skewer inserted in the centre comes out clean.
7. Ten or so minutes before the end of the baking time, prepare the drizzle. Put the blood orange juice and the golden caster sugar into a small saucepan and heat gently, not stirring the mixture.
8. Once all the sugar has dissolved, allow the mixture to simmer over a medium heat for 2 to 3 minutes, again resisting any temptation to stir.
9. The mixture will thicken and become syrupy, at which point remove from the heat.
10. Once the cake is cooked, remove it from the oven and place (still in its tin) on a wire cooling rack.
11. Quickly pierce small holes all over the top of the hot cake with a skewer and pour the warm syrup evenly over the top.
12. Allow the cake to cool completely before removing it from the tin.

SNOWDROPS

When night-time bars me in
and I am sitting sewing
my fancy takes the whim
to think of snowdrops growing.

They sprinkle grudging places
with slender drops of white,
and hang their orphan faces
in narrow hoods of light.

So frail I must recall
the shoulder of the cloud,
the scratching of the squall,
the wind, the frost, the flood.

Child kindness of the year
young promise of beguilement
more tender and more dear
than old fulfilment,

how strange it is to see
and hard to understand
your silver shine like charity
in winter's stubborn hand!

    Margiad Evans (1909–1958)

The Thrushes and Blackbirds have been singing me into an idea that it was Spring, and almost that leaves were on the trees. So that black clouds and boisterous winds seem to have mustered and collected in full Divan, for the purpose of convincing me to the contrary...

The thrushes are singing now as if they would speak to the winds, because their big brother Jack, the Spring, was not far off.

John Keats (1795–1821), from a letter to George and Thomas Keats, 21 February 1818

Life is already tingling with the irresistible urge of a new season, tingling in every jointed thorn twig, tingling through the air-filled quills of the cock chaffinches, whose feathers each day grow brighter and brighter.

Let the frost return, let the snow fly past our windows and pile itself in drifts against the hedges, we remain unintimidated. It is February, and to-morrow or the next day the sun will be shining again upon the sprouting leaves of the lords and ladies, and upon the first shining gold of the earliest celandines.

Llewelyn Powys (1884–1939), from *The Twelve Months*, 1936

The aconites under my blenheim orange apple out early this year, but pale and peaky as if the sun was not strong enough to colour a flower a right yellow, but they look nice with their little green frills round their necks and I was glad when I saw them for when the aconites open I know that the snowdrops will soon be here and then we shall have the daffies and the wallflowers and know that its [*sic*] spring.

Flora Thompson (1876–1947), from *Still Glides the Stream*, 1948

Flooded pools and saturated ground have deterred most of the walkers. I think myself alone, crossing the waterlogged stretch between estuary and sea, looking only at the mosses, golden and fluffed up, threaded softly through the sodden grass. My eyes have been fixed low, but something causes them to rise. One small lift of the head and I have landed somewhere else, in another realm entirely, where time forgets to flow and birds are made of gold.

I watch the golden plover on the ground before me, basking in the shining plumage. The brilliant sparks, scattered flames roaring in brown relief, seem to enact a special alchemy before my eyes – there is gold being made, here, in this living bird. When I am able to leave the speckled fire of the feathers, I look into its eyes. With its head tilted and slender build, it is not as cocksure as I would expect the owner of living gold to be. It is not quite sure what to do with itself, and nor am I. I could live in this moment for days.

Elizabeth-Jane Burnett (1980–), from *Country Diary*,
published in *The Guardian*, 23 February 2023

Among the last year's brown ruins, heaped together by the wind in the hedgerows, she found the fresh green crinkled leaves and pale star-like flowers of the primroses. Here and there a golden celandine made brilliant the sides of the little brook that (full of water in 'February fill-dyke') bubbled along by the side of the path; the sun was low in the horizon, and once, when they came to a higher part of the Leasowes, Ruth burst into an exclamation of delight at the evening glory of mellow light which was in the sky behind the purple distance, while the brown leafless woods in the foreground derived an almost metallic lustre from the golden mist and haze of the sunset.

Elizabeth Gaskell (1810–1865), from *Ruth*, 1853

THAW

Over the land freckled with snow half-thawed
The speculating rooks at their nests cawed
And saw from elm-tops, delicate as flowers of grass,
What we below could not see, Winter pass.

      EDWARD THOMAS (1878—1917)

INDEX OF AUTHORS

A
Aiken, Joan 237
Alcott, Louisa M. 149, 211
Angelou, Maya 169
Arkell, Reginald 123
Arnim, Elizabeth von
  Elizabeth and Her German Garden 57, 66, 123, 199
  The Enchanted April 48
  Princess Priscilla's Fortnight 83
Arnold, Matthew 73
Auden, W. H. 6
Austen, Jane 157
  Emma 82–3, 88, 218
  Mansfield Park 22
  Persuasion 173
  Pride and Prejudice 134
  Sense and Sensibility 58, 59, 136–7

B
Barker, Elspeth 182
Bates, H. E. 90
Bell, Adrian 161, 191
Bell, John 7
Bertelsen, Aaron 156
Binyon, Laurence 176–7
Blackmore, R. D. 178, 236
Blake, William 15
Bloom, Valerie 142, 213
Blythe, Ronald 191

Boston, Lucy M. 211
Braddon, Mary Elizabeth 133
Bridges, Robert
  'The Garden in September' 135
  'January' 233
  'North Wind in October' 160
  'Spring Goeth all in White' 47
Brontë, Anne 16, 64
Brontë, Charlotte
  Collected Poems 118
  Jane Eyre 106–7, 182, 228
Brontë, Emily
  'The Bluebell' 56
  'Fall, Leaves, Fall' 159
  'Loud without the Wind was Roaring' 117
  Wuthering Heights 116
Brooke, Rupert 84–5
Brooks, Gwendolyn 95
Browning, Robert 41
Buchan, Anna Masterton 57
Burnett, Elizabeth-Jane 147, 167, 242
Burnett, Frances Hodgson 48, 90
Burns, Robert 192
Butler, Octavia 6

C
Campbell, Nancy 211
Carr, J. L. 88, 125
Cather, Willa 194

Christie, Agatha 237
Clare, John 68, 150, 220–1
Cocker, Mark 230
Coleridge, Hartley 185
Coleridge, Samuel Taylor 172
Collins, Wilkie 182
Congreve, Celia 208–9
Cooper, Susan Fenimore 18, 82, 158, 190
Cope, Wendy 219
Coulthard, Sally 147
Cowper, William 134
Crompton, Richmal 64

D

Davies, W. H. 130
Deakin, Roger 115, 230
Delafield, E. M. 211, 231
Dickens, Charles 125, 216–17
Dickinson, Emily 89, 127, 189
Dodge, Mary Mapes 74–5
Dodgson, Charles 6
Dods, Margaret 67, 116, 157, 226
Don, Monty 123, 145
Donne, John 193
Douglas, O. 57
Drinkwater, John 148
du Maurier, Daphne 115
Dunbar, Paul Laurence 35

E

Eliot, George 6, 9, 158
Adam Bede 22
The Mill on the Floss 199, 210
'Roses' 104
Scenes of Clerical Life 86
Ellis, Alice Thomas 28
Emerson, Ralph Waldo 234
Erasmus 7
Evans, Margiad 240

F

Farley, Paul 196
Field, Rachel 146
Forster, E. M. 6
Fuller, Claire 88

G

Gaskell, Elizabeth
  Cranford 36–7, 59
  Ruth 242
  Wives and Daughters 161, 174
Gates, Nicholas 147
Gill, Nikita 23, 164
Godden, Rumer 88
Grahame, Kenneth 16, 106, 115, 215
Gray, Thomas 87

H

Hardy, Thomas
  Far from the Madding Crowd 16, 178–9
  'The Oxen' 214

Tess of the d'Urbervilles 62
The Woodlanders 22, 147, 184
Harrison, Melissa 30
Hart-Davies, Christina 59
Hartley, Dorothy 59
Hayden, Eleanor G. 138
Heath, Ambrose 156
Herford, Oliver 223
Herrick, Robert 227
Higginson, Thomas Wentworth 40
Hill, Susan 207
Holden, Edith 230
Hood, Thomas 114
Hopkins, Gerard Manley 50
Housman, A. E. 25
Howard, Elizabeth Jane 88
Howitt, Mary 139
Hudson, W. H. 31, 174
Humble, Kate 156

I

Irving, Washington 210

J

James, Henry 77, 113, 161
Jefferies, Richard
   Bevis 67, 168
   Hodge and His Masters 102, 190
Jekyll, Gertrude 78, 113
Jerome, Jerome K. 99, 115
Johnson, Anna Rose 211
Johnstone, Christian Isobel 67, 116, 157, 226
'Julian' 40

K

Kay, Jackie 20, 200
Keats, John 98, 132, 241
Kilvert, Reverend Francis 43, 61, 138, 231
   Kilvert's Diary 230
Kimmerer, Robin Wall 88
Knight, India 30
Komachi, Ono No 175

L

Landon, Letitia E. 49
Larcom, Lucy 32–3
Laughton, Freda 52
Lawrence, D. H.
   'Letter from Town: the Almond Tree' 29
   The Rainbow 67, 118–19, 215
Leighton, Clare 137
Lewis-Stempel, John 147
Lister-Kaye, John 232
Locke, John 7

M

Macdonald, Benedict 147
McDowell, Marta 123
MacNeice, Louis 131
Mandanna, Sangu 182
Mansfield, Katherine 95

Martin, Violet Florence 19
Marvell, Andrew 122
Meijer, Eva 59
Meredith, George 24
Milton, John 6
Mitford, Mary Russell 31, 37, 133, 195
Mitford, Nancy 30
Montgomery, L. M.
   Anne of Green Gables 34, 48, 133, 168
   The Blue Castle 30, 180, 198
Moore, Thomas 109
Morpurgo, Michael 230
Morris, William 143

N
Nesbit, Edith 19, 30, 136
Netherclift, Beryl 194–5

O
Oliphant, Margaret 180

P
Pilcher, Rosamunde 237
Plumley, Gavin 147
Powys, Llewelyn 152, 184, 241

R
Ransome, Arthur 115
Read, Miss 91
Rebanks, James 30

Roberts, Julius 156
Rossetti, Christina 94, 188
Rossetti, Dante Gabriel 69, 183

S
Sackville-West, Vita 14
Setterfield, Diane 182
Shakespeare, William 19, 235
Shelley, Percy Bysshe 46
Shoel, Thomas 229
Sissay, Lemn 11
Smith, Dodie 48
Smith, Sydney 207
Somerville, Edith 19
Somerville & Ross 19
Stafford, Fiona 48
Stevenson, Robert Louis 181
Struther, Jan 178
Sukegawa, Durian 48
Sutton, Paula 123
Swift, Katherine 123

T
Taber, Gladys 61
Tagore, Rabindranath 103
Teasdale, Sara
   'August Moonrise' 126
   'Dusk in Autumn' 166
   'May Day' 60
   'A Winter Blue Jay' 202–3
Tennyson, Alfred, Lord 110–12, 225

Thaxter, Celia 72
Thomas, Edward
  'Digging' 171
  'First Known When Lost' 10, 201
  The Heart of England 34, 51, 119, 144, 162, 228
  'Sowing' 38
  'Thaw' 243
Thompson, Flora
  Candleford Green 64
  Lark Rise 86, 145
  Lark Rise to Candleford 59
  Over to Candleford 36
  Still Glides the Stream 241
Thoreau, Henry David 18, 149
Trollope, Anthony 76
Turner, Charles Tennyson 92
Tynan, Katharine 163

U

Uttley, Alison
  Ambush of Young Days 51
  The Country Child 211, 218
  Recipes from an Old Farmhouse 156
  A Year in the Country 91, 152

W

Wallis, Velma 237
Waters, Sarah 182
Webb, Mary 39, 124
Weisgarber, Ann 237
Wharton, Edith
  Ethan Frome 198, 237
  The House of Mirth 144
  Hudson River Bracketed 28
  Summer 76–7
White, Gilbert 136
Whittier, John Greenleaf 81
Wilde, Oscar 6
Wood, Laura 115
Woodforde, James 37, 66, 230
Woolf, Virginia 6, 134, 172, 232
Wordsworth, Dorothy 27, 162
Wordsworth, William
  'I Wondered Lonely as a Cloud' 26
  'Lines Written in Early Spring' 17
  A Night in June 79
  'The Prelude' 206
  'To a Butterfly' 97
Wylie, Elinor 151

Y

Yassin, Warda 80
Yates, Lucy H. 156

GENERAL INDEX

A
almonds: winter glögg 212
animals and their young, names of 53
apples
  apple varieties 153
  baked apples 154–5
autumn 128–85

B
birds, collective nouns for 197
biscuits: lavender shortbread 120–1
blood orange drizzle cake 238–9
books to read
  in autumn 147, 156, 182
  by the water 115
  for cosy evenings by the fire 211
  for the country cook 156
  for a country cottage 59
  for the country diarist 230
  for the country gardener 123
  as the mist thickens 182
  as the sap rises 30
  in spring 30, 48, 59
  in summer 88, 115, 123
  in the sunshine 88
  under an apple tree 147
  under the cherry blossom 48
  when the snow falls 237
  in winter 211, 230, 237

C
cake, blood orange drizzle 238–9
cheese: wild garlic & three cheese scones 54–5
chocolate, indulgent hot 165
cinnamon: rose petal & cinnamon tea 105
commonplace books
  definition of 6
  history of 7–8
  how to keep 8–9
country contentments
  autumn 140–1
  spring 44–5
  summer 100–1
  winter 204–5
country wisdom
  autumn 170
  spring 42
  summer 93
  winter 222

D
drinks
  honey for tea 94
  indulgent hot chocolate 165

rhubarb gin 21
rose petal & cinnamon tea
    105
winter glögg 212

F
flowers, summer wildflowers to
    spot 108

G
garlic: wild garlic & three
    cheese scones 54–5
gin, rhubarb 21
glögg, winter 212

H
honey for tea 94
hot chocolate 165

L
lavender shortbread 120–1

O
oranges
    blood orange drizzle cake
        238–9
    winter glögg 212

R
raisins
    baked apples 154–5

winter glögg 212
red wine: winter glögg 212
rhubarb gin 21
rose petal & cinnamon tea 105
rum: winter glögg 212

S
scones, wild garlic & three
    cheese 54–5
shortbread, lavender 120–1
spring 12–69
sultanas: baked apples 154–5
summer 70–127

T
tea
    honey for tea 94
    rose petal & cinnamon tea
        105

V
vodka: winter glögg 212

W
wild garlic & three cheese
    scones 54–5
wildflowers, summer 108
winter 186–243

SOURCES

'Late October' from JUST GIVE ME A COOL DRINK OF WATER 'FORE I DIIIE: POEMS by Maya Angelou, copyright © 1971 by Caged Bird Legacy, LLC. Used by permission of Random House, an imprint and division of Penguin Random House LLC. All rights reserved. Reproduced with permission of the Licensor through PLSclear.

H. E. Bates, extract from *My Uncle Silas* (1939), published by Penguin Books.

Extract from *A Countryman's Autumn Notebook* © Adrian Bell. Reproduced with kind permission of the Eastern Daily Press.

'Autumn Gilt' and 'Christmas Carol' © Valerie Bloom, 2000, from *The River's a Singer: Selected Poems* (Macmillan). Reprinted by permission of Eddison Pearson Ltd on behalf of Valerie Bloom.

Extract from *Borderland: Continuity and Change in the Countryside* © Ronald Blythe. Published by Canterbury Press, Norwich (2007).

Extract from *Maud Martha* © Gwendolyn Brooks, 1953, published by Faber & Faber Ltd. Reprinted by consent of Brooks Permissions and Faber & Faber Ltd.

Elizabeth-Jane Burnett, extract from 'Country Diary', published in *The Guardian*, 23 February 2023. Copyright Guardian News & Media Ltd 2024.

Elizabeth-Jane Burnett, 'Ginger Spice' from *Twelve Words for Moss*, published by Penguin. Copyright © Elizabeth-Jane Burnett, 2023. Reprinted by permission of Penguin Books Limited.

J. L. Carr, extract from *A Month in the Country*, published by Penguin Classics (1980).

Wendy Cope, 'The Christmas Life' © Wendy Cope, 2024, from *Collected Poems* (Faber & Faber Ltd). Reprinted with permission of Faber & Faber Ltd.

Extract from *Family Roundabout* © Richmal Crompton, 1948. Reproduced with permission of Persephone Books.

Extract from *The Ivington Diaries* by Monty Don reprinted by permission of Peters Fraser & Dunlop (petersfraserdunlop.com) on behalf of Monty Don.

Margiad Evans, 'Snowdrops' from *Autobiography*. Published by Calder Publications (1974).

Paul Farley, extract from 'Robin' from *The Mizzy*. Published by Picador (2019).

'On the First Flowers of Spring' and 'On the First Leaves of Autumn' © Nikita Gill, 2022, from *These are the Words* (Macmillan Children's Books). Reproduced with kind permission of David Higham Associates.

Susan Hill, extract from *Through the Kitchen Window*. Published by Hamish Hamilton (1984).

Jackie Kay, extract from 'The World of Trees' © Jackie Kay, from *Darling: New & Selected Poems* (Bloodaxe Books, 2007). Reprinted with permission of The Wylie Agency.

Jackie Kay, 'Life Mask' © Jackie Kay, from *Darling: New & Selected Poems* (Bloodaxe Books, 2007) by permission of the publisher. Reproduced with permission of Bloodaxe Books. www.bloodaxebooks.com

Ono no Komachi, 'Seeing the moonlight' from *The Ink Dark Moon: Love Poems by Ono no Komachi and Izumi Shikibu, Women of the Ancient Court of Japan*, translated by Jane Hirshfield with Mariko Aratani, translation copyright © 1986, 1987, 1988, 1989, 1990 by Jane Hirshfield. Used by permission of Vintage Books, an imprint of the Knopf Doubleday Publishing Group, a division of Penguin Random House LLC. All rights reserved.

Freda Laughton, 'Now Linnet' from *Transitory House* by Freda Laughton, published by Jonathan Cape. Copyright © Freda Laughton, 1945. Reprinted by permission of The Random House Group Limited.

Clare Leighton, extract from *The Farmer's Year*, © Estate of Clare Leighton. All rights reserved 2025.

Extract from *Gods of the Morning* © John Lister-Kaye 2016, published by Canongate Books. Reproduced with permission of the Licensor through PLSclear.

Louis MacNeice, extract from 'Autumn Journal' © Louis MacNeice 2013, published by Faber & Faber Ltd. Reproduced by kind permission of David Higham Associates.

Miss Read, extract from *The English Vicarage Garden* (introduction). Published by Michael Joseph (1988).

Vita Sackville-West, extract from 'The Land' © Vita Sackville-West. Reproduced with permission of Curtis Brown Group Ltd, London on behalf of The Beneficiaries of the Estate of Vita Sackville-West.

Lemn Sissay, 'We are wildflowers' © Lemn Sissay, 2023, from *Let the Light Pour In: Morning Poems* (Canongate Books). Reproduced with permission of the Licensor through PLSclear.

Gladys Taber, extract from *Stillmeadow Seasons* (1950).

Extract from *Home Life* by Alice Thomas Ellis reprinted by permission of Peters Fraser & Dunlop (petersfraserdunlop.com) on behalf of the Estate of Alice Thomas Ellis.

Alison Uttley, extract from *The Country Child*. Published by Puffin Books (1931).

Extracts from *A Year in the Country* © Alison Uttley, 1957 and *Ambush of Young Days* © Alison Uttley, 1937. Reproduced with kind permission of the Society of Authors as the Literary Representative of the Alison Uttley Literary Property Trust.

Warda Yassin, 'Swift' from *More Fiya: A New Collection of Black British Poetry*. Published by Canongate Books (2022).

Batsford is committed to respecting the intellectual property rights of others. We have taken all reasonable efforts to ensure that the reproduction of all contents on these pages is done with the full consent of the copyright owners. If you are aware of unintentional omissions, please contact the company directly so that any necessary corrections may be made for future editions.

FURTHER READING

For more information on commonplace books, please see the following resources:

- My website (mirandsnotebook.com) for free articles and guides to keeping a commonplace book.
- *The Notebook: A History of Thinking on Paper* by Roland Allen. Profile Books, 2023.
- *How Romantics and Victorians Organized Information* by Jillian M. Hess. Oxford University Press, 2022.

ACKNOWLEDGEMENTS

With gratitude and thanks to the fabulous Batsford team, especially Polly Powell, Nicola Newman, Bella MacConnol, Eoghan O'Brien, Sanya Jain, Mia Autumn Roe, Jane Pickett and Frida Green. Thank you as well to Nikki Ellis for your work on the layouts.

Thank you to Debbie Powell for your illustrations which add so much beauty to the book.

To all my YouTube, Substack and Instagram friends: thank you so much for your support and lovely comments over the years! This book is for all of you who have enjoyed my literary recommendations and book reviews, and I hope it offers plenty more bookish inspiration for you to appreciate throughout the seasons.

An extra big thank you to my Seasons of Story members, who make so much of my online work possible, and who were the first to hear about my very first book. I appreciate every one of you!

Thank you to Alison Ball, Andrea Conner, Jane McMorland Hunter and Janelle McCulloch for your friendship and encouragement.

And finally, all my heartfelt love, thanks and gratitude to my mum, Donna Mills, who will always be my number one cheerleader.

ABOUT THE AUTHOR

Miranda Mills is a writer and YouTuber who shares book reviews, seasonal reading guides and insights into country life on her social media channels. Miranda is the founder of Seasons of Story, an online literary journal and community celebrating literature, art and the natural world. She can be found on mirandasnotebook.com, Instagram @mirandasbookcase and YouTube @MirandaMills. She lives in Yorkshire.